LIBRARIANS OF 1
AND SCHOOLS OF EDUCATION

BRINGING THE PAST TO LIFE

A survey of prize-winning and other outstanding historical
stories for children.

Part 1- Pre-history to 1750.

compiled by

Alasdair Campbell and Deborah Gibbons
with help from some members of the L.I.S.E. Group.

2002.

Cover illustration from *The Shield Ring*
by Rosemary Sutcliff.
Illustrated by C. W.Hodges,1960 ed.
Published by permission of Oxford University Press

ISBN: 0 901922 36 6

Design & print by Cg 01792 390813

CONTENTS

INTRODUCTION

Value of Historical Novels

There will always be different opinions about the value of fiction as an aid to the study of history. Certainly some children do develop an interest in history during their school years, either through classwork or the school library or from home influences. Interest is one thing, the factual content of history is another, and some teachers believe that fiction by its very nature can be dangerously misleading. Others maintain that the possible benefits far outweigh any risks. Among the enthusiasts is Grant Bage, now at the Cambridge School of Education, who has argued recently that:

"A storied history curriculum ...offers historical stories as memorable and emotional investments which may - or may not - yield unpredictable returns from a lifelong future". (1)

Whatever the differences of opinion, almost everyone would agree that if children are to gain something useful from historical novels, they must be given access to good quality material. What adults need is a simple way of tracing the best historical novels, those which are well-researched, inspiring and readable at different age-levels. In this booklet, as with others in the same series, it is assumed that the most reliable guidance comes from the several annual awards for excellence in children's literature, of which the Carnegie Medal is the best-known in this country - see Appendix 1. Normally selection panels for awards announce a shortlist and later a single winning title: experience has shown that the short-listed titles are of much the same calibre as the winner, which may well be chosen on the basis of compromise. All the authors whose work is listed here - with the notable exception of Geoffrey Trease - have been at least shortlisted for major awards in Britain or America. A high proportion of the books themselves are prizewinning or shortlisted titles. This booklet from the L.I.S.E. Outstanding Children's Books Project is the first of two which between them are intended to cover the whole stretch of history from its earliest beginnings to the period within adult memory.

Historical Novels in Children's Literature

Historical novels go back to the earliest children's literature, and one or two, like Marryat's *The children of the New Forest* or Twain's *The prince and the pauper,* have survived for many generations. However, after the Victorian period and even after the first literary prizes were awarded in the inter-war period, historical fiction in England was for many years of generally poor quality - though Geoffrey Trease did begin writing in 1934. The first revival came in the 1950s, when Rosemary Sutcliff and Cynthia Harnett led the way, with Harnett's The wool pack winning the Carnegie Medal in 1951. A very large number of historical novels appeared during the next twenty-five years, many of them high quality. Rosemary Sutcliff certainly dominated the scene, but writers like Ronald Welch, Mollie Hunter, Leon Garfield and Barbara Willard came to the fore while Trease continued his long writing career without much recognition.

In the 1970s historical writing for children began to go out of fashion in England - less so in America - and no historical novel has won the Carnegie Medal in the last two decades. Long historical novels on the Sutcliff model have always seemed to lack appeal for the average young reader, so the growth of child-centred methods of education may have encouraged authors and publishers to turn away from history, and 'political correctness' may also have been a factor. Whatever the reasons for the rather sudden decline in historical writing, there are indications of a new revival in the late 1990s, with perhaps less demanding material and an increasing use of the time-shift method of bringing the past to life. A new study of the genre, in the form of a collection of relevant articles, appeared in 2001. (2) As it happens, historical fiction for adults has flourished at all levels during the past quarter-century .

Categories of Historical Novel

As already indicated, all the titles included in this booklet and its intended sequel have been selected for their literary quality and historical reliability. All have been published since 1950, and in this booklet all are written by British or American authors. For the periods between 1066 and 1750, the emphasis is on British history. A very few books dealing with history of other cultures after 1066 have been shortlisted for awards, but not enough to provide any reasonable balance: and the two National Curriculum Key Stage 3 periods from 1066 to 1750 are related to developments in Britain.

Traditionally historical novels have featured the great events of history with the action centred around real people, often monarchs or major historical figures. Such novels are well represented in this booklet, but equally prominent are those concerned with social history, including what might be called period novels. Mere historical romances or ill-researched 'costume' novels are unlikely to have been considered for awards. Time-switch novels, increasingly favoured by good writers in the last decade, do present some problems. When Janet Fisher produced a comprehensive annotated list of some 450 historical novels in 1994, (3) she excluded time-shift novels altogether on the grounds that they always include an element of fantasy. That is true, but in some cases the time-shift mechanism is not obtrusive and the historical elements are of a high standard, as for instance in Ronald Welch's *The gauntlet* or Susan Cooper's *King of shadows*. About half a dozen good quality time-shift stories are included in this booklet. Other varieties of fantasy found in historical stories such as an ability to foresee the future may be acceptable in small doses, but if the action of the story depends vitally on some supernatural power, there must be a large question mark against it.

Short story writing is a mode which seems to have little appeal for the leading historical writers, and in this booklet is represented only by Barbara Willard's *The keys of Mantlemass*. For collections of stories covering all periods of history, see Appendix 2. Two other categories of fiction relevant to this booklet may be mentioned here. Suitable illustrations can sometimes do wonders to enliven history, and in the Post-War decades even books for older readers often carried the work of fine artists like Charles Keeping or Walter Hodges. Nowadays only books designed for the younger age-ranges are well-illustrated: an excellent example is Richard Platt and Chris Riddell's *Castle Diary*, 1999, which has a thirteenth century setting and was shortlisted for at least two awards.

Finally the category of novels presented in diary or journal form, such as Karen Cushman's *Catherine, called Birdy*, has become increasingly popular in recent years and has obvious advantages in the context of historical writing.

Arrangement and layout of this booklet

Even in these times of National Curriculum history there is a widespread belief that children in Britain can go through the whole of their schooldays without acquiring much idea of national chronology. In this L.I.S.E. booklet the arrangement is chronological, with the hundred-odd selected titles divided into eight sections starting with the pre-historic period. Within each section, one or sometimes two titles which seem particularly outstanding have been selected as 'lead' novels, and at the end of each section any titles that are obviously intended for younger readers have been grouped together. Reading ages are always difficult to determine, and many novels designed primarily for readers at secondary school ages could be read by younger children; at the end of each entry in this booklet there is a note suggesting the most likely reading ages. Lead novels are those which "ally a powerful imagination to historical awareness" (4) and are mostly either recent prize-winners or very well-known.

Apart from the 'lead' novels, titles within each section are listed in chronological order as far as possible. Some titles - those set in the Dark Ages, for instance - are difficult to date precisely, and some others are listed as part of a sequence. Ronald Welch's unique series of ten novels about members of the Carey family in different periods are generally given brief entries at the end of each section. Other writers whose work appears in four or more sections are Rosemary Sutcliff, Henry Treece and Geoffrey Trease. Details given for each title listed are the author's surname and first forename, the first British publisher and the date of the original publication. Many of the earlier titles have been re-issued, sometimes more than once, and sometimes with different publishers. Prices of editions available are constantly changing. Unfortunately some publishers allow even the most notable books to go out of print very quickly, though the work of prize-winning authors is possibly the least likely to suffer in this way. Many out-of-print books are, of course, available in school or other education libraries and may often be obtained on loan through public libraries.

References:

1. Bage G. Narrative matters: teaching and learning history through story. Falmer, 1999.

2. Collins, F and Graham, J. (eds). Historical fiction for children: capturing the past. Fulton, 2001.

3. Fisher, J. An index of historical fiction for children and young people. Scolar Press, 1994.

4. King, C. The historical novel- an underused resource. *Teaching History.* 51, April 1988, pp.24-26.

THE OUTSTANDING CHILDREN'S BOOKS PROJECT.

The main objects of the Outstanding Children's Books Project have been to bring together librarians working in teacher education who have a common interest in children's books, to encourage co-operative activities and to publicise worthwhile books for children. *Outstanding Children's Books* was published by L.I.S.E. in 1990, followed by *Commended Books for Under-Twelves* in 1994, *Commended Books for Over-Tens* in 1995 and *Outstanding Sequence Stories* in 1998. A ten-year supplement to the first publication, called *From Goggle-Eyes to Harry Potter*, was published in 1999. This new booklet is the first of two dealing with outstanding historical stories.

Thanks are due to members of the L.I.S.E. group and others who have assisted with these publications, especially Deborah Gibbons, formerly of the Cheltenham and Gloucester College of Higher Education - now the University of Gloucestershire. Others who have given particular help with this booklet are Kathryn Smith of Canterbury Christchurch University College and Rosemary Smith of the University of Plymouth. On the production side, valuable assistance has been given by Madeleine Rogerson, L.I.S.E.'s Publications Officer at the University of Wales Swansea, and her colleague Jane Phillips.

Alasdair Campbell.
Formerly Education Librarian, University of Keele.
February 2002.

SECTION A - PRE-HISTORIC TIMES AND VERY EARLY HISTORY

Setting a children's novel in pre-historic times is clearly a demanding task, but several outstanding writers did make the attempt in the boom years after World War 2. *Warrior scarlet,* although outside Rosemary Sutcliff's favoured Roman period, did much to establish her reputation. In more recent years Peter Dickinson has shown a particular interest in a time when records were non-existent.

Lead Novel:

Sutcliff, R. Warrior scarlet, 1958. (Carnegie Medal shortlisted).

Others at Secondary school level:

Dickinson, P. A bone from a dry sea, 1992. (Carnegie Medal and Whitbread Award
shortlisted).
Dickinson, P. The Kin, 1998. (Carnegie Medal shortlisted).
Swindells, R. When darkness comes, 1973,(Re-issued 1993).
Treece, H. The dreamtime, 1967.
Sutcliff, R. Sun horse, moon horse, 1977.

Primary School Level:

Sutcliff, R The chief's daughter, 1967.
King, C. Stig of the dump, 1963.

LEAD NOVEL:

1. SUTCLIFF, Rosemary. Warrior scarlet. Oxford U.P, 1979.

An introductory note from the author tells us that this story of early community life and ritual is to be dated to about 900 B.C., set in the Suffolk Downs area. The central character is Drem, aged nine at the start, whose damaged right arm makes it difficult for him to gain acceptance as a warrior. He becomes a skilful left-handed spearsman, but fails to kill his wolf at the first ritual attempt. Relegated to the inferior status of a shepherd, he has to guard the flock at lambing time and finally manages to kill the very same wolf when it attacks. He is welcomed back to the ranks of the warriors and at the end, aged sixteen, he is ready to marry the despised daughter of a travelling bronze-smith.

Apart from its quality as a taut adventure story, this novel provides valuable insight into the life-style of a Bronze Age person. The vast importance of weather to a farming and hunting community, the separation of men and women for most purposes and the rigid social barriers enforced in these communities are among the more prominent themes. One striking episode features the first arrival of iron in a community accustomed only to bronze.

Age range: 11 to 15.

OTHERS AT SECONDARY SCHOOL LEVEL:

2. DICKINSON, Peter. A bone from a dry sea. Gollancz,1992.

The inspiration for this fairly complex story appears to have been news of a particular theory of human evolutionary development to which the author refers in a note at the end of the book. The novel is constructed in twenty-four alternating sections, twelve dealing with a present-day research expedition in Central Africa, and twelve with the life of an early human community existing millions of years before in the same area which at that time bordered an inland sea. The two narratives are linked by the finding of a significant bone in the modern period, and in each of them a strong female character acts decisively.

In the pre-historic period the people are virtually sea-creatures, expert at swimming and never venturing far from the water. The community is male-dominated, but one young girl, Li, begins to think in an original way and, with the help of some dolphins, shows the leader how to carry his people forward. Since linguistic communication is assumed to be rudimentary at the time, the narrative has to proceed with minimal use of dialogue throughout. A stimulating read for anyone with an interest in the several theories of pre-historic evolution.

Age range: 14 upwards.

3.DICKINSON, Peter. The Kin. Macmillan, 1998

An imaginative work telling the story of a group of children in Africa when finding food and shelter were vital for survival. The book is split into four sections, each continuing the story from the perspective of a different member of the group, and each chapter is followed by the sort of tale early folk told around the fire, explaining creation and the patterns of society.

The children search for Good Places to live, and adapt to new circumstances as they join a group in a volcanic crater, and learn to fish and follow tricky paths through marsh reedbeds. They are inventive, and one of them, who is physically disabled, first devises two animal traps and then the plan which saves them from the greatest danger of all - demon men. The spirit world plays an important place in their lives and another member of the group with psychic powers is able to go into a trance and pass on messages from their animal guardian, Moonhawk.

This is a book full of rich descriptions and imagery, and though it is a work of the imagination, you feel at the end of it as if you have a far better idea of life as it might have been lived in early times.

Age range: 12 and upwards

4. SWINDELLS, Robert. When darkness comes. Brockhampton, 1973

In the distant past a hunter gatherer community eking out an existence in some inhospitable woodland region is endangered by rivalry and ambition. The teenage boys Morc and Gyre are forced to part when Gyre's reckless father Gawl leads a rebellion against the tribal chief. The rebels are expelled but gain possession of a vital flint-producing area. Both groups are then threatened by the appearance of a more advanced group with better weapons. They manage to defeat the newcomers by trapping them in a forest fire, and after the death of Gyre decide to re-unite and move from the woodlands to a hilly area nearby.

This is a fairly bleak story with ample violence, but the teenage characters are interesting and the background detail convincing. The book's title is an apt one, since the author frequently refers to the perils of the night and shows how much the lives of early human communities were affected by changing seasons and patterns of weather.

Age range: 11 to 14

5. TREECE, Henry. The dream-time. Brockhampton, 1967.

The lame boy known as Crookleg is regarded with contempt and suspicion in his community, the Dog People, partly because of his fondness for drawing rather than fighting. After the death of his mother in childbirth and his father in a skirmish he leaves his community and wanders from one group to another, often earning admiration for his artistic skills but generally failing to persuade others that a peaceful life-style is better than continuous warfare. After a time he meets up with a community of peaceful cave-dwellers who decorate their walls with charcoal drawings. Most of them are killed by a wolf-pack, but Crookleg, now known as Twilight, escapes with the girl Blackbird and an orphan baby, eventually settling with another less warlike community.

Although Treece deliberately mingles several different

periods of antiquity, he does manage to convey an entirely convincing impression of early peoples struggling to survive, and at the same time raises important issues about contrasting life-styles and attitudes. His sombre style and pared-down language seem just right for the subject, as also does Charles Keeping's range of slightly unfinished-looking illustrations.

Age range: 10 to 14.

6. SUTCLIFF, Rosemary. Sun horse, moon horse. Bodley Head, 1977

A short novel with a complex theme, powerfully written but perhaps too demanding for most young readers. The central character is Lubrin Dhu, third son of a chieftain, whose artistic temperament is unsuited to an era of superstition and inter-community violence. In the end Lubrin gives himself up for sacrifice beside the Uffington white horse which he has created, in order that his enslaved people may go free. Based on a lifelong interest in the period and a knowledge of its manners and rituals.

Age range: 14 upwards.

PRIMARY SCHOOL LEVEL

7. SUTCLIFF, Rosemary The chief's daughter. Macmillan, 1967.

Ten-year-old Nellan is the daughter of an early British chief at a time when marauding raiders from Ireland are a constant menace. She has befriended an Irish boy prisoner, Dara, and is determined to help him when the community's water supply fails and he is condemned to be sacrificed. Dara escapes and Nellan is herself condemned to death, but in escaping Dara has accidentally restored the flow of water and its re-appearance saves her at the last moment.

Ms Sutcliff tells a simple story with plenty of excitement and few complexities, and the historical background is sketched in with her usual skill and attention to detail. The illustrations are by

Victor Ambrus, who received the Kate Greenaway Award in 1965 and 1975.

Age range: 8 to 11.

8. KING,Clive. Stig of the dump. Penguin,1963.

Not strictly speaking an historical nor even a time-shift story, since the whole of the action takes place in present-day Sussex. However, the Stone Age-survival boy Stig does give eight-year-old Barney some idea of how people lived in ancient times, while in the last two chapters Barney and his elder sister Lou have a vision of summer solstice ceremonies in a Stone Age encampment, including the erection of standing stones. This story could serve as a useful introduction to ancient history for young readers, who will surely enjoy the humour and excitement which the author builds up from the contrast between Stone Age and modern life-styles. Illustrated by Edward Ardizzone.

Age range: 8 to 11.

SECTION B - ANCIENT CIVILISATIONS: EGYPT, GREECE AND THE MIDDLE EAST

Ancient Greece has long been regarded as the starting-point for European history and features prominently in the National Curriculum at Key Stage 2. Arguments about the Trojan War, long simmering amongst historians, have again broken out in 2001. Apart from Adele Geras's recent novel there have been surprisingly few prize-winners in this area, though several notable writers are perhaps unlucky to have missed out. For the Middle East and Egypt there are some interesting titles available at all levels.

Lead Novel :

Geras, A. Troy, 2000. (Whitbread Award winner).

Others at secondary school level :

Harris, R. The moon in the cloud, 1968. (With two sequels).
Dickinson, P. The blue hawk, 1976. (Guardian Prize winner).
Fyson, J. The three brothers of Ur. 1964.
Fyson, J. The journey of the eldest son. 1965.
Renault, M. The lion in the gateway. 1964. (Re-issued 1993).
Lillington, K. Young man of morning, 1979.
Trease, G. The crown of violet, 1952.

Primary school level :

Turnbull, A. The Queen cat. 1998.
McCaughrean, G. Casting the Gods adrift, 1998.
Treece, H. The windswept city, 1967.
Trease, G. Mission to Marathon, 1997.
Sutcliff, R. The truce of the Games. 1971.

LEAD NOVEL:

1. Geras,Adele. Troy. Fickling/Scholastic,2000

A longer-than-average novel, apparently based on careful research, dealing with the closing episodes of the siege of Troy, c. ll90 B.C., including the violent deaths of the Trojans Laocoon and Hector and the famous Greek strategem of the Wooden Horse.

Two main characters are the sisters Marpessa, handmaid to Helen, and Xanthe, a nurse in the Blood Room for wounded Trojan soldiers. Two young men, Alastor and Iason, are also prominent throughout, and there is a large supporting cast of Trojans involved in the war. The end of the siege and the ransacking of Troy are described in graphic detail. The two sisters survive the slaughter and leave Troy with the prospect of more peaceful futures.

The mythology of the Trojan War is of course an established feature of European culture, and in this novel Zeus, Aphrodite, Poseidon and other Gods sometimes appear alongside the human characters. The historical thread is never neglected, however, so that the musings of Zeus can serve to remind the reader that trading rivalry, as much as the abduction of Helen, had served to inflame the Greek leaders. A demanding novel for experienced readers, full of memorable set-pieces.

Age range : l4 upwards

OTHERS AT SECONDARY LEVEL:

HARRIS, Rosemary 2.The moon in the cloud. Faber, 1968
3. The shadow on the sun. Faber, 1970
4. The bright and morningstar.Faber,1972.

The three closely-related stories in this series have major elements of fantasy, and they have sometimes been seen as most suitable for readers at primary school leyel. However, each story is quite long and complex, and between them they provide a comprehensive picture of courtly and priestly life in the earlier centuries of Kemi, otherwise Ancient Egypt. In an introduction to the first volume the author states that she had in mind a date of c.2200 B.C.,the period of the sixth dynasty of the Old Kingdom, which may also have been the approximate date of the biblical Flood. The leading character in all three stories is the Canaanite animal-trainer Reuben, who joins Noah in the Ark and later becomes a trusted helper at the court of the young Egyptian King Merenkere.

Each story is packed with high adventure, much of it resulting from priestly intrigue and ambition. Alongside the dramatics there is plenty of detail about society in this distant period of history: the pervasive religious rituals, the elaborate marriage ceremonies, the general enthusiasm for fine buildings and even the early practice of tomb-robbing, now so fully evidenced through modern discoveries.

Age range : 10 to 15.

5. DICKINSON, Peter. The blue hawk. Gollancz,1976

This prize-winning novel deserves a mention for its striking portrayal of life in a priest-dominated society which bears a strong resemblance to Ancient Egypt, though never formally identified as such. The young teenager Tron with his tamed hawk is a notable character. The period might be anywhere in the 3000-year history of the Nile civilization, in which some factors, such as the hazards of travel through the desert or by river, remained virtually unchanged. A book which might well inspire an interest in the ancient civilizations, but perhaps too unspecific to serve as background reading for historical studies.

Age range:12 to 16.

Fyson, Jenny. 6.The three brothers of Ur. Oxford U.P., 1964
7.The journey of the eldest son. Oxford U.P.,1965

There is no trace of either mythology or fantasy in these two stories set in Sumeria about 2000 B.C., both of which were shortlisted for the Carnegie Award. The first story introduces the family of a wealthy Chaldean merchant living in the highly civilised city of Ur. Young teenager Shamashazir is the responsible eldest son, who is obliged to cope with the follies of his younger brothers,and comes to realise that he has a destiny to fulfil.

In the second, rather livelier, story Shamashazir sets out from Ur on a hazardous trading mission. In the course of many adventures he passes through communities practising several forms of idolatrous worship and becomes convinced of the existence of one omnipotent God. He returns to Ur as a hero, capable of leading his people towards a new faith. Few readers will realise that the adventurous storyline is centred on one of the major turning-points of history, the coming of monotheism;in an Epilogue the author explains that Shamashazir is based on the Old Testament character of Abraham. Whatever Ms Fyson's personal beliefs, there is no obvious Christian propaganda here, nor any other overt didacticism.

Age range: 12 to 15.

8. RENAULT, Mary. The lion in the gateway. Kestrel 1964. (Re-issued 1993)

Mary Renault was a distinguished writer of adult novels with a particular interest in Ancient Greece and the growth of democracy. Here she employs her literary skills in a largely factual narrative of the great events of the fifth and sixth centuries B.C. in Greece, Asia Minor and Persia up to the Battle of Plataea in 479 B.C. All the characters who appear- among them Hippias, Leonidas, Themistocles, Darius and Xerxes - are real figures from history, with only their thoughts and words imagined.

The chapter devoted to the last stand of the Spartans at Thermopylae under Leonidas in 480 B.C. is a particularly fine piece of writing, imaginative yet historically accurate. Supplementary features include a map of the area in the time of Xerxes,a list of dates and an explanatory note referring to early historical sources. There is also an extended glossary and a comprehensive index. Nevertheless this work is usually classed as fiction.

Age range: 10 upwards.

9.Lillington, Kenneth. Young man of morning. Faber,1979.

Lillington is now known for contemporary fantasies such as *Ash-blonde witch* or *Jonah's mirror*, while his satirical comedy *Josephine,* set in the 1930s was shortlisted for the Guardian Award in 1989. There is no element of fantasy or satire in this story, which has a background of the Greek struggle for survival against Persia, culminating in the Battles of Thermopylae and Salamis in 480 B.C. The main fictional characters are Philip, a naturally gifted healer, and his friend Lucy, a flute-girl.

Written to fill what the author saw as a gap in available literature, while he was teaching a class of eleven-year-old boys.

Age range: 11 to 14
.

IO. Trease, Geoffrey. The crown of Violet. Macmillan, 1952.

This story is set in the same century B.C. as Lillington's novel, but seven or eight decades later, during the life-times of Socrates and Plato who were probably born in 469 and 427 respectively. This was not a peaceful time for the Athenians, and the story includes the unfolding of a plot against the state although the main emphasis is on domestic and cultural matters. Teenager Alexis, growing up in a conventional Athenian family, develops a relationship with socially-suspect Corinna in the face of parental disapproval, and competes secretly in a play-writing competition. After various adventures and contacts with the famous philosophers he wins the drama prize and can look forward to a successful future.

The author here shows his usual skills in building up a convincing historical picture, in this case of Greek culture and society, while at the same time providing a fast-moving adventurous narrative. Character-drawing is not exactly Trease's forte, but with Alexis and the other Athenian characters he has producedsome of his best creative work. Illustrated by C.W.Hodges.

Age range: 11 to l4.

PRIMARY SCHOOL LEVEL

11. TURNBULL, Ann. The Queen cat. Macdonald,1989

A fully illustrated story of just forty-six pages, which
clearly belongs to Ancient Egypt in the era of cat-worship, perhaps
about 1500 B.C.; the author never refers to date or country. The
central character is Neferet, known as Men-Sheri, daughter of a
goldsmith living in the city of Bubastis, with two elder sisters
already serving as priestesses. The city is in mourning after the
death of its sacred Queen Cat. Men-Sheri goes with her father by
Nile-boat to Memphis, where she finds a stray cat which is later
identified as the new Queen. A simple story about ordinary people
but pleasantly written and with interesting background detail of
things like a water-side inn and river travel. The illustrative
drawings by Jan Lewis fully support the text in its portrayal of life
in town and country.

Age range: 6 to 8

**12. McCAUGHREAN, Geraldine. Casting the gods adrift. Black,
1998.**

Black's Flashbacks series, to which this title belongs, is
specifically designed to support classwork and includes suggestions
for further reading of fiction and non-fiction. However
McCaughrean is an experienced historical writer with creative gifts,
and here she contrives an intriguing short thriller with a setting of
Egypt, in the fourteenth century B.C. Family matters are central,
but there is a strong background of priestly and religious practice
with sidelights on the dynasty of Pharaohs and a late reference to
Tutankhamen. Illustrated.

Age range : 8 to 12

13. TREECE, Henry. The windswept city. Hamilton, 1967.

Treece's version of the Trojan War's climax is much
shorter than that of Geras (see lead novel, above) and also more

down-to-earth. The story is in fact de-mythologised, with no Gods overlooking the scene and the outcome depending on human endeavour and ingenuity - though some legendary incidents like Cassandra's warning are included. The central character is Asterius, a young slave-boy, who serves Helen and in the course of his work meets most of the Trojan leaders. He also encounters Agamemnon,who is shown with human weaknesses and some good qualities. After the fall of Troy, c.1190 B.C., Asterius joins the surviving Hittite warriors who have latterly given support to the Trojans. Treece provides a list of characters, a factual note on modern knowledge of Troy and several maps of the area. While in no way playing down the savagery of war, he has clearly kept in mind the needs of younger readers. Illustrated.

Age range : 9 to 12.

14. TREASE, Geoffrey. Mission to marathon. A & C Black, 1997

This shortish story based on the dramatic events of 490 B.C. in Greece is another in the Flashbacks series from Black. Trease mentions Pheidippides as a noted runner but does not make him a major character. The action is seen mainly through the eyes of a schoolboy, Philip, who is sent to Marathon to warn relatives of an impending attack by the Persians under Darius. In describing the Athenian tactics devised by their commander, Miltiades, Trease keeps strictly to the known facts. His account of the battle itself is vivid but fairly restrained with the roles of the Athenians, Plataeans and Spartans clearly stated. A fairly typical story from this author, exciting and informative but peopled largely with stereotyped characters.

Age range: 9 to 11.

15. SUTCLIFF, Rosemary. The truce of the Games. Hamilton, 1971

This is one of Sutcliff's most sucessful stories for younger children, set in the classical Greece of the fifth century B.C., after the threat of invasion from Persia had receded. Athens and Sparta were deadly rivals and frequently at war, but both allowed their leading athletes to compete in the Games held periodically at Olympia. Amyntas from Athens and Leon from Sparta, both older teenagers, meet while in training for the Games, and become friends for a few weeks. They race against each other in the proper sporting spirit, knowing that they may next meet on some battlefield. The situation is calculated to make readers think about the nature of friendship and patriotism and, without ever seeming didactic, the author also manages to suggest something of the contrasts between Athenian and Spartan life-styles. In spite of the main characters being teenagers, this book is clearly designed for the younger age-ranges.

Age range: 8 to 11.

SECTION C – EARLY BRITAIN AND THE ROMAN EMPIRE, 55B.C. - 407A.D.

For more than forty years in the post-war period Rosemary Sutcliff was the dominant figure in historical writing for children, and a favourite with the Carnegie Award judges among others. Some of her best work was concerned with Roman Britain, and many of these novels are still widely available. Henry Treece, though perhaps better known for his Viking stories, was also drawn to some of the great events of Roman Britain. Rome itself, and different aspects of the Empire, have provided varied themes for some other leading writers.

Lead novels:

Hunter, M. The stronghold, 1974. (Carnegie Medal winner).
Sutcliff, R. The mark of the Horse Lord, 1965. (Phoenix Award winner).

Others at secondary school level:

Sutcliff, R. The Eagle of the Ninth, 1954. (Carnegie Medal shortlisted).
Sutcliff, R. The silver branch, 1957 (Carnegie Medal shortlisted).
Sutcliff, R. Frontier wolf, 1980.
Sutcliff, R. Song for a dark queen, 1978. (Re-issued 1996).
Treece, H. The Queens's brooch, 1966.
Speare, E. The bronze bow, 1961. (Newbery Award winner).
Trease, G. Word to Caesar, 1956.

Primary school level:

Treece, H. War dog, 1962.
Sutcliff, R. The eagle's egg, 1981.

LEAD NOVELS:

1.Hunter, Mollie. The Stronghold. Hamilton, 1974.

This story is set in the Orkney islands around the beginning of the Christian era, or perhaps a little earlier. The central character is Coll, aged eighteen at the start, who suffers from a permanent hip injury but is a natural innovator. There are two linked elements in the plot – Coll's plan to develop a new type of defence against the marauding Roman slave-gatherers, and the bitter conflict between the local tribal chief Nectan and the senior Druid in the area, Domnall. After many experiments Coll succeeds in building a tower which provides security against the Roman Pirates, and an uneasy truce is agreed between Nectan and Domnall.

In a Foreword to her book, the author refers to her particular interest in the unique Orcadian brochs, and to her theory about their origin. Two diagrams are provided. She has obviously made a careful study of ancient Orcadian society, yet this is not a didactic book. In one aspect it is an exciting adventure story with plenty of suspense, in another there is an interesting view of the conflict between superstition and rational thinking. The female characters, though quite well-drawn, are all subsidiary.

Age range: 12 to 15.

2.Sutcliff, Rosemary. The mark of the Horse Lord. Oxford University Press. 1965.

An ex-gladiator in the adventure of his life. A story of treachery and changed identity, loyalty and the growth of responsibility. This vivid story is set in Roman Britain, c. 240 A.D., on the desolate northern border of England with Scotland. The richness of language and metaphor brings the scenery alive and evoke the times as though we still lived in them. The lives of Phaedrus, the gladiator, and Midir, the Lord of the Daldriads, become inextricably linked when Phaedrus assumes Midir's identity. We are introduced to characters as diverse as Liadhan, the traitorous Royal Woman, and Conory, with his wild, ferocious pet cat. Phaedrus is tested to the limit as the story builds to an exciting and unexpected climax.

On the surface this is a richly told tale of adventure, love, war and treachery. However, it is far more complex than that and introduces the reader to issues of character building, team building, kingship and family.

Age range: 10 to 14.

OTHERS AT SECONDARY SCHOOL LEVEL:

3.Sutcliff, Rosemary. The Eagle of the Ninth. Oxford University Press, 1954.

This is the first of several novels featuring members of a Romano-British family, the Aquilas, in different periods of British history. The first hero, Marcus, appears in the mid-second century A.D. when, as a former centurion invalided out of the army, he decides to set out for the distant Northern areas of Valentia and Calendonia. His mission is to seek information about the fate of his father's legion, the Ninth, which had disappeared completely in 117 A.D. Accompanied by a freed slave, Esca, he enters Druid/Pictish territory and retrieves the legion's battle standard. Pursued by vengeful tribesmen, the two men escape across the Roman Wall and return to Marcus's family home near Winchester.

This is primarily an adventure story, with a fair sprinkling of coincidences and high drama, but the backgrounds of life in Roman Britain and in Caledonia are filled in with skill and enthusiasm. The author knows about food, weapons, religious customs, primitive medicines and much more. She is impressively knowledgeable without ever seeming to lecture.

Age range: 11 to 14.

4.Sutcliff, Rosemary. The silver branch. Oxford University Press, 1957.

The events of this story take place in the years 293 to 297, when Britain was under the control of two self-proclaimed local emperors, Carausius and Allectus. Ms Sutcliff portrays Carausius, a half-Irish former naval commander, as a benign dictator, the victim of treachery by Allectus, who employed Saxon mercenaries. Allectus himself ruled harshly for three years, until defeated and executed by the Roman general Constantius Chlorus.

The chief fictional characters here are the cousins Flavius and Justin, descendants of Marcus from the previous novel. They are loyal military supporters of Carausius who are forced into hiding after his murder and become involved with a group of Christians and others working to overthrow Allectus. The closing chapters are mainly concerned with the savagely contested warfare in southern England in 296, when the invading Roman armies were mauled at Silchester but just managed to save London from destruction. This story is quite closely related to the known history of the period, though dates are not mentioned in the text and place-names like Calleva or Rutopiae are generally left for the reader to identify.

Age range: 11 to 14.

5.Sutcliff, Rosemary. Frontier wolf. Oxford University Press, 1980.

This third episode from the Aquila family's eventful history was completed and published nearly two decades after the second, and is decidedly more adult in tone than the others. There are no coincidences or youthful escapades here, and the first half of the book is slow-moving. It should appeal particularly to those with an interest in Scottish history, since the author pays great attention to the complex tribal system and patterns of social behaviour among the Celts. There is action enough in the second half of the story when the tribes unite in a rebellion and Alexius Aquila has to organize a fighting retreat across the Scottish borderlands. The date is around 340 – 343 A.D. The Emperor Constans, second son of Constantine, did in reality lead a campaign against the Celts in 343, and in this story he appears as a character in the last chapter. Unusually for Rosemary Sutcliff, she prefaces this text with a factual note of explanation.

Age range: 12 to 15.

6.Sutcliff, Rosemary. Song for a dark queen, Hodder and Stoughton,1978. (Re-issued 1996).

As its title suggests, this story of the British queen Boudicca from her childhood up to her death in 61 A.D. is certainly one of Ms Sutcliff's darker novels. Through the eyes of the bard Cadwan we see Boudicca growing up as a princess of the Iceni tribe, married at the age of thirteen to Prasutagus and sharing the leadership of the tribe for some twenty years of semi-independence under a tolerant Roman regime. When Nero becomes emperor in 54 A.D. the situation changes, and soon the Iceni are fighting to survive and avenge their wrongs. Boudicca, half-maddened with grief and fury, leads them to some successes but is finally routed by the disciplined Romans. A terrible massacre follows, and Boudicca commits suicide. Some of these later events are vividly described in letters sent home by the young soldier Agricola, afterwards governor of Britain, but in general the Romans are seen here as ruthless oppressors of the freedom-seeking Britons. Selected for the anti-traditional Other Award in 1979.

Age range: 14 to 16.

7. Treece, Henry. The Queens's brooch. Hamilton, 1966.

Another view of Boudicca and the Iceni rebellion, less sympathetic towards the Iceni and more inclined to depict them as brutal people. The central character here is Marcus Volusenus, who first appears at the age of seven when he joins his Tribune father in Britain. Ten years later he is in the thick of the fighting as Boudicca and her ferocious warriors defy the equally ruthless Romans for a time. After the crushing of the 61 A.D. rebellion, described in full gory detail, Marcus and the Saxon girl Gerd are desperate to escape from war-torn Britain and decide to seek a more peaceful life-style in Alexandria. In this late novel, Treece has dispensed with his usual background note, but he makes his points plainly through occasional inserted comments and through his main characters.

Age range: 12 to 15.

8. Speare, Elizabeth. The bronze bow. Gollancz, 1961.

This story is set in Galilee, at the time of Jesus, when the Romans ruled as conquerors. Daniel, a young Galilean, has just cause to hate the Romans and is acutely aware of his Jewish heritage and the obligations it brings. As a teenager he joins the Zealots, involving many of his friends in rebellion in the process. Parallels are drawn between his life and the life of a rich noble family. Tragedy inevitably ensues. Daniel is confused by both the teachings of Jesus and the attitude of his sister, Leah, towards the Romans. Eventually he himself comes to see that guerrilla warfare is not the answer to everything .

This is a powerful story which brings Jesus and his teachings to life indirectly but very effectively. At the same time, issues of loyalty, friendship and violence are explored in a readily accessible way. Equally valuable for historical or religious studies.

Age range: 10 to 14.

9. Trease, Geoffrey. Word to Caesar. Macmillan, 1956.

Fifteen-year-old Paulus recounts his adventures in Britain, Gaul and Rome in 117/118 A.D. the year when Hadrian succeeded Trajan as Emperor. His story begins with his narrow escape from a barbarian incursion into Cumbria, continues with a stay in peaceful Roman Bath and a hazardous sea and land journey to Italy, and finishes with a series of dramatic escapades in Rome. While trying to deliver a vital message to Hadrian, he outwits some murderous villains with the help of resourceful Antonia, and at last looks forward to further travels around the empire in Hadrian's entourage.

As always, Trease is adept at providing a strong historical background and plenty of factual information without ever breaking up the narrative flow. Background details in this story include the value of Caligula's lighthouse at Boulogne, the horrific slaughter of animals in the Roman arena, the techniques of chariot racing, the appearance of a scholar's library of scrolls, and the problem of corruption in the Roman Civil Service. The later chapters contain many descriptive passages, generally short and vivid, dealing with the buildings and landscape of imperial Italy. There are twelve illustrations.

Age range: 10 to 14.

PRIMARY SCHOOL LEVEL:

10. Treece, Henry. War dog. Brockhampton, 1962.

In contrast to some of his rather demanding stories for his older readers, Treece here provides a straightforward narrative centred on the fortunes of a British war dog, Bran, at the time of the main Roman invasion of Britain in 43 A.D. Bran at first serves with his British master, Gwyn, but after Gwyn is killed he passes into the hands of a Roman soldier, Marcus Titus. Marcus later leaves Britain for Gaul and finally Rome, and Bran goes with him to become a family pet. A good quota of background detail is provided and several historical persons appear, including the Celtic leader Caractacus and the Roman general Vespasian. An author's note at the end of the book provides further historical information about the period. Numerous illustrations by Roger Payne.

Age range: 8 to 11.

11. Sutcliff, Rosemary. The eagle's egg. Hamilton,1981.

This very simple story is presented as a tale told by the former Roman soldier Quintus to his grandchildren. He describes how, as a young standard-bearer based in Eboracum (York) in c. 80 A.D., he had fallen in love with a British girl, Cordaella, but under Roman regulations was too young to marry. Soon he joined Agricola's expedition into Scotland, where by quick-thinking he helped to avert a mutiny, and later acquitted himself well at the Battle of Mons Graupius in 84 A.D. Promoted to centurion rank ahead of expectations, he returned to York to claim Cordaella as his bride. Includes background detail of the military and civilian life at the time, with illustrations by Victor Ambrus.

Age range: 7 to 10.

SECTION D – THE DARK AGES AND THE VIKINGS, 407 – 1066

Anyone writing about the Dark Ages has to contend with the difficulty of dividing off a mass of myth and legend from the shadowy framework of reality, and also with the fact that pitiless violence was endemic throughout Europe at the time. Nevertheless, several good children's writers, and Henry Treece in particular, have chosen the period as a suitable background for their work.

Lead Novel:

Sutcliff, R. The lantern bearers, 1959. (Carnegie Medal winner).

Others at secondary school level:

Sutcliff, R. Dawn Wind, 1961.
Atterton, J. The last harper, 1983.
Furlong, M. Wise child, 1987.
Carter, P. Madatan, 1974. (Re-issued 1987).
Treece, H. The Viking saga, 1955 – 1960.
Branford, H. The fated sky, 1996.
Hodges, C. W. The namesake, 1964 and The marsh king, 1967.
Peyton, K. Firehead, 1998.
Treece, H. The last of the Vikings, 1964.

Primary school level:

Price, S. The saga of Aslak, 1995.

LEAD NOVEL:

1.Sutcliff, Rosemary. The lantern bearers. Oxford University Press, 1959

This is one of Sutcliff's most sombre narratives, full of tragedy, treachery and sorrow, as well as plentiful background detail. The period covered is that of the two decades after the last Roman troops left in 407 A.D. It was a time of almost continuous confused warfare, involving British Romans, Celtic tribes and a variety of invaders including Saxons, Jutes and Irish Scots. Apart from providing a skeleton map of fifth century Britain, the author does nothing to put her story in context and seems to take for granted some knowledge of the period and its shadowy personalities.

The central character is a British-born Roman soldier, Aquila, aged eighteen in 407, who decides to stay in Britain. He is promptly enslaved, but later escapes to join the Celtic irregulars in Wales. While campaigning he meets several historical/legendary characters such as Vortigern and the British High King Ambrosius. Towards the end of the novel Ambrosius's nephew Artos, otherwise Arthur, features as a brilliant leader in battle. The many-sided character of Aquila gives the story an essential core of humanity, and his struggle to maintain standards at a time of violent upheaval should appeal strongly to thoughtful readers.

Age range: 14 to 16.

OTHERS AT SECONDARY SCHOOL LEVEL:

2.Sutcliff, Rosemary. Dawn Wind. Oxford University Press, 1961.

A story covering about twelve years in the later sixth century A.D., another in the author's loosely related series featuring members of the Romano-British Aquila family – but not obviously connected with *The lantern bearers*. The hero this time is Owain, a young Christian Briton of Roman descent, who appears first as sole survivor of a battle near Bath in which the invading Saxons have triumphed. Owain makes his way to the great Roman settlement of Viroconium (Wroxeter), now derelict, and there meets a young girl called Regina. For her sake he chooses slavery with a Saxon family and goes with them to their farm in Sussex. After ten years of faithful service he is given his freedom and goes north again to be re-united with Regina.

Although the sixth century was a time of continuous warfare, the author is here concerned to show that individuals could lead relatively normal lives and keep their personal loyalties while adapting to enforced changes. She also stresses her view of Christianity as a civilizing influence - the dawn wind – and paints a sympathetic portrait of Augustine, who arrived in Kent with his missionary monks in 596 A.D.

Age range: 12 to15.

3. Atterton, Julian. The last harper. MacRae, 1983.

Atterton was seen by some critics as a natural successor to Rosemary Sutcliff and this novel was shortlisted for a Young Observer Teenage Fiction prize. It is certainly reminiscent of Sutcliff in one of her sterner moods, with the emphasis on heroic endurance through prolonged struggle and suffering. The story is told by Gwion, aged fourteen in Chapter 1, whose tribe in the Celtic kingdom of Bryneich on the North Sea coast is decimated by invading Angles. He finds a refuge in the Carlisle area, but after a few years returns with a temporarily unified army of Celtic tribes, led by Urien, to storm the fortress of Bamburgh. Soon afterwards the tribes start to quarrel among themselves and lose any chance of permanent victory over the Angles (later the English) who have retreated to Lindisfarne. The closing chapters are fairly cheerless, but Gwion has survived one disaster after another and resolves to use his ballad-writing skills to commemorate Urien's heroic campaign. The author appears to have done his research well and presents a vivid, highly-coloured portrait of the chaotic conditions in northern England during the sixth century.

Age range: 14 to 16.

4. Furlong, Monica. Wise child. Gollancz, 1987.

This seventh century story is set mainly on the Isle of Mull, then part of Dalriada, with a background featuring the conflict between early Christian beliefs and the ancient Celtic culture of nature worship. The story is told by the young girl known as Wise Child, who in the absence of her parents is entrusted to the care of Juniper, a strong-minded Cornishwoman practising herbal medicine and inclined to challenge accepted male hegemony. After a severe winter and an outbreak of smallpox Juniper is accused of witchcraft, but she and Wise Child both escape to a new life away from Mull.

Whatever one may think about the semi-supernatural powers ascribed to Juniper and the black magic apparently practised by her enemies, there is much to be learnt here about Scottish society in the Dark Ages. The hardships of everyday life and the terror of afflictions such as leprosy are duly emphasised, but perhaps the most memorable scene-painting comes when Wise Child attends a Beltane Feast and takes part in the terrifying but fairly harmless ceremonies derived from pagan tradition.

Age range: 11 to 14.

5. Carter, Peter. Madatan. Oxford University Press, 1974. (Re-issued 1987).

The central character here is Madaah who, as a young teenager living in the Outer Hebrides in the late eighth century, is kidnapped by marauding Norsemen from Orkney. He goes with them on another raid to Northumbria, escapes after a shipwreck and spends some years with Christian monks in York and elsewhere before making his way back to the Hebrides. Madaah's progress reflects to some extent the author's interest in religion and the growth of civilized thinking, but violence and cruelty were endemic at the time and at a personal level Madaah is beset with treachery and vengeance. There are no child or female characters and no light relief, but the story is well told with convincing background detail.

Age range: 12 to 15.

6a, b, c. Treece, Henry. The Viking saga. Penguin/Bodley Head,1985.

The three parts of this book were originally published separately as *Viking dawn* (1955), *The road to Miklagard* (1957) and *Viking sunset* (1960). They recount the travels and adventures of Harald Sigurdson, first as a boy of fifteen, then as a warrior of twenty and finally in middle years as a leader of men, the starting dates being 780, 785 and 815 respectively. Each part has an introductory note by the author and a map showing the Vikings' extensive journeyings round a large area of the world. From his home fjord in Norway Harald and his war-band sail to parts of Scotland, Ireland and the Mediterranean as the Vikings of the time certainly did; and finally, in line with a theory of the author's, they go west and join the American Indians in a climactic orgy of violence.

The Dark Ages were indeed a time of continual warfare, brutal oppression and superstition. Treece knew all about these aspects, and does full justice to them. He was also a great admirer of the Icelandic Sagas, and particularly in the third part of this trilogy, he draws on their liveliness and humour for the conversation of his characters. A dominant character in the second and third parts is the gigantic Caledonian Grummoch, who not only provides good entertainment but is the only significant figure surviving in the end. Treece is quite ruthless with his male characters and rarely bothers to develop his females.

Age range: 11 to 14.

7. Branford, Henrietta. The fated sky. Hodder Children's Books, 1996.

This is the story of Ran, a child of the Vikings, growing up in Norway probably in the ninth century. Her father has been drowned, and she is taken by her mother and a cruel stranger called Vigut to celebrate the winter festival with neighbours. Her mother is killed by wolves on the way, and Ran is chosen to be the sacrifice to Odin. She escapes with a blind musician called Toki and they journey to Iceland to make a life together. However Vigut also comes to Iceland and their peaceful life together ends in a bloody raid.

The writer gives us a vivid impression of life in Scandinavia, when the Norse gods ruled and hardship and death were all too common. We see the landscape clearly through Ran's descriptive words, and suffer with her when her children are threatened.

Setting a tale in Viking times is fairly unusual, and has worked very well in this case. We get a good insight into the life led by the women left behind whilst the men go off trading and adventuring on their boats, often never to return.

Age range : 10 to 14 years.

8. Hodges, C. Walter. The namesake. Bell, 1964.

Alfred Dane-leg, struggling through many hardships on one leg, is the namesake of the Saxon prince who became King of Wessex and achieved lasting fame as Alfred the Great. As narrator, the lesser Alfred covers the period from the martyrdom of King Edmund in 870 to the destruction of the southern Viking fleet in a storm in 877. A narrative dealing with the great events of the ninth century must inevitably have its full quota of violence, cruelty and treachery, but in this story there is also some emphasis on the influence of Christianity, and especially on the piety and wisdom of King Alfred. Alfred is portrayed as a man devoted to religion and learning, not physically strong, who perforce makes himself a master of fighting tactics.

Thoughtful readers may profit from some quite philosophical passages as, for instance, when Alfred takes his followers to Stonehenge and speaks to them about its symbolic meanings. By contrast, some of the battle narratives are memorably vivid, especially when illustrated by the writer in his alter ego as a noted artist. 9. Shortlisted for the Carnegie Medal, 9. *The marsh king* (Bell, 1967) is a sequel in the same vein, but somewhat lacking in imaginative power.

Age range: 14 to 16.

10. Peyton, Kathleen. Firehead. Scholastic,1998.

In this story set mainly in East Anglia in the early eleventh century, the author lays some stress on the confused mixture of European racial groups in England at the time. Her central character Edmund Firehead grows up in a Saxon family but his actual father was a red-haired Celtic minstrel. Edmund too has red hair, and this unusual feature helps him to survive when the invading Vikings ransack his settlement. He becomes a serf in the Viking chieftain's household, befriended by some of its members and hated by others.

The author does full justice to the brutality and violence which were endemic in England at the time. Edmund's friend and fellow serf Sigy has his left hand chopped off and thrown to the dogs for trying to escape, and is later murdered in cold blood. Edmund shows equal ruthlessness in avenging him, but earns favour with the Vikings and is finally allowed to marry the chieftain's daughter, Estrid. A powerful story which includes occasional references to national events, such as the death of King Aethelred and the accession of Cnut (Canute) in 1016.

Age range: 12 to 16.

11. Treece, Henry. The last of the Vikings. Brockhampton,1964.

Treece was particularly interested in the Vikings and their voyages, but most of his stories are set in the years of greatest Viking activity from the eighth century to the tenth. The title of this story is appropriate since it covers the mid-years of the eleventh century and has for its hero Harold Hardrada, who led the invading Norwegians at the Battle of Stamford Bridge in 1066. Most of the book is concerned with Harold's memories of his long career in Scandinavia and elsewhere. Not all of his memories are warlike, for Harold also recalls such interludes as a tax-gathering expedition in Russia and his courtship of Elizabeth, a spirited Russian princess.

The Battle of Stamford Bridge and the death of Harold are featured in the final chapter. The defending English army was, of course, led by the other Harold, son of Godwin, who was himself killed at the more famous Battle of Hastings in the same year.

Treece's preference for the Norwegian Harold is typical of his individual approach to pre-Norman history, but as always he writes with conviction and a real feeling for the Viking way of life. Illustrated by Charles Keeping.

Age range: 12 to 15.

PRIMARY SCHOOL LEVEL:

12. Price, Susan. The saga of Aslak. A & C Black, 1995.

It is probably very difficult to write a cosy story about life in the late ninth century, and this one, although it belongs to the well-illustrated Flashbacks series for younger readers, is certainly not cosy. Aslak and his sister Astrid grow up in Norway in the household of a Viking raider, but are separated when Astrid is sold as a slave to Denmark. Aslak vows to free her, but is himself enslaved and taken to Britain in 876. There he prospers, but Astrid dies in childbirth, leaving an infant daughter for Aslak to bring up as his own. The narrative flows smoothly through seven short chapters, without light relief but also without undue emphasis on the savagery of the times. The complex relationships of Norse people and Saxons and the clash between Norse traditions and Christianity are prominent in the last four chapters, but are expressed in the simplest possible terms. There are two outline maps and suggestions for further reading.

Age range: 9 to 12.

Section E – British History, 1066 to 1300

National Curriculum History, Key Stage 3, starts, like so many other things, at 1066. The early mediaeval period, though by no means lacking in violence, does provide opportunities for those who prefer domestic settings and evidence of progress in human affairs. The American prize-winning writer Karen Cushman is one who favours the period for her novels featuring strong female characters. Kevin Crossley-Holland is an experienced writer now turning to historical work, while for younger readers *Castle diary* (Platt and Riddell) is a recent gem.

Lead novels:

Crossley-Holland, K. Arthur; the seeing stone, 2000. (Guardian Prize winner and Whitbread Award shortlisted).
Cushman, K. The midwife's apprentice, 1995. (Newbery Award winner).

Others at secondary school level:

Sutcliff, R. Knight's fee, 1960
Sutcliff, R. The shield ring, 1956. (Carnegie Medal shortlisted)
Welch, R. Knight crusader, 1954. (Carnegie Medal winner)
Tomlinson, T. The forestwife, and two sequels, 1993-2000
Crossley-Holland, K. Arthur; at the crossroads, 2001. (Sequel to come)
Hendry, F. Quest for a maid, 1988
Cushman, K. Catherine, called Birdy, 1994

Primary school level:

Platt, R. and Riddell, C. Castle diary, 1999.
Sutcliff, R. The witch's brat, 1970.
Boston, L. The stones of Green Knowe, 1976

LEAD NOVELS:

1. Crossley-Holland, Kevin. Arthur; the seeing stone. Orion, 2000

In its primary aspect this is an historical novel covering a year in the life of young Arthur de Caldicot, son of a landowner in Shropshire, near the Welsh border, who at the age of thirteen is beginning to question some of the injustices of mediaeval society. The year is 1199, and on the national scene John becomes king on the death of his brother Richard I. In an introductory note the author refers to his extensive research, and acknowledges debts to experts on topics such as the weapons, food and farming practices of the mediaeval period.

Intended as the first volume of a trilogy, the book is made up of a hundred short chapters, most of them centred on young Arthur's life at home with his family. The picture is a fairly bleak one including harsh realities such as debilitating illness, the death of children and brutal punishments for minor offences. At the end Arthur discovers some family secrets and prepares to leave home in search of glory as a soldier on the Fourth Crusade. There is a small fantasy element in the book, with a character called Merlin helping Arthur to look back in time to the legendary boyhood escapades of King Arthur.

Age range: 13 to 15

2. Cushman, Karen. The midwife's apprentice. Macmillan, 1995

The central character of this book has nothing, not even a name, at the beginning of the story. She is just a waif and stray, travelling from settlement to settlement, stealing, or working to get enough food to keep her alive. When the midwife takes her in she gains a roof over her head, but is made to work hard for her keep. As her life develops more security she learns about herbs and natural remedies, and picks a name for herself, Alyce. Her growing confidence is tested when she fails to deliver a baby and runs away, humiliated. She finds a new home and gradually recovers until she feels strong enough to return to her apprenticeship.

A vivid picture is painted of village life during the reign of Edward I, especially from the point of view of outcasts, struggling to find enough bread and water to keep themselves alive. Life was harsh then and this story provides us with plenty of information whilst also telling an involving, and sometimes highly entertaining, tale.

Age range: 10 to 14

OTHERS AT SECONDARY SCHOOL LEVEL:

3. Sutcliff, Rosemary. Knight's fee. Oxford U.P., 1960

Among Sutcliff's many historical adventure stories none perhaps is more solidly based in the facts of British history than this one. The period covered is from 1094 to 1106, an eventful time both in Britain and Normandy, which is summarised by the author in an historical note at the end of the book. She also refers in the text to many of the major events, such as the Welsh rebellions, the start of the First Crusade, the second crowning of William II in 1099 and his mysterious death in 1100. In the closing chapters she involves her main characters in Henry Ist's campaigns in Normandy, culminating in his decisive victory at Tinchebrai in 1106. The facts of history are never obtrusive, the main interest being centred on a rags-to-riches style hero with friends and enemies.

From humble beginnings as a half-Saxon kennel-boy at Arundel Castle, Randal finds favour in a Norman household, is knighted after Tinchebrai and returns to Sussex as a manorial lord. His experiences en route include the glamour of a Norman marriage celebration and the fury of a witch-hunt used as cover for attempted murder. Illustrated by Charles Keeping.

Age range: 11 to 14

4. Sutcliff, Rosemary. The shield ring. Oxford U.P., 1956

Though covering almost the same period of history, starting in 1090, this story is markedly different from *Knight's fee;* the whole action takes place in the Lake District, where according to tradition – supported by some evidence – a band of Norsemen resisted the conquering Normans until well into the reign of Henry I. The story is told from the point of view of the Norsemen and their Saxon allies, with the Normans seen as barbarous enemies whose superior strength is nullified by the rugged Lakeland terrain. Main characters apart from the Norse warriors are Bjorn, distant descendant of the Roman Aquila family, and Frytha, a Saxon girl who escapes from a Norman massacre and grows up in the Norse stronghold. The Norse people pursue trading and farming activities whenever possible, but inevitably there is almost continuous warfare including desperate single combats and the torturing of captives. In many respects this is a near-adult novel, though the ending is certainly hopeful.

Age range: 12 upwards

5. Welch, Ronald. Knight crusader. Oxford U.P., 1954.

A novel which puts the emphasis on military history and features an all-male cast of characters would probably not be considered for anyone's literary award nowadays. Nevertheless *Knight crusader* was a worthy winner of the Carnegie Medal some fifty years ago, and it can still be recommended as a readable and informative introduction to the Crusades era in Britain and the Middle East. *Knight crusader* is divided into three parts, the first two set in Outremer, the Crusaders' Christian enclave, and the third in twelfth century Wales. The central character is Philip D'Aubigny, born in Outremer of Welsh descent and aged seventeen when the story begins in 1185. Philip becomes a soldier and survives many escapades, including a period of captivity, before arriving in Wales to claim his inheritance. Among the historical figures appearing are Saladin and Richard I, enemies in the Third Crusade, but treated quite impartially by the author. Welch as always concentrates on the narrative and the period detail carefully avoiding any bias in matters of political or religious controversy.

Age range: 10 to 14

6-8. Tomlinson, Theresa. 1. The forestwife. MacRae, 1993. 2. Child of the may. MacRae, 1998. 3. The path of the she-wolf. Red Fox, 2000.

To those readers who enjoy Theresa Tomlinson's realistic stories of British working-class life in the last hundred years or so, this rather unrealistic trilogy may come as a surprise. Set in the reign of Richard I and John from about 1192 to 1216, the three stories amount to a re-telling of the Robin Hood legends, with Maid Marian in the leading role. Marian, herself a skilled archer, refuses to marry Robert the Hooded and sets up a makeshift hospital in the forests, where she and her female helpers minister to the sick and homeless. Robert and his henchmen are either in deep depression or strutting about with bows and arrows. Whether it makes sense to re-write the old Sherwood legends in such politically-correct terms is a matter of opinion, but the background of national turbulence and local oppression is sketched in convincingly enough with plenty of gory detail.

Age range: 12 to 15

9. Crossley-Holland, Kevin. Arthur; at the crossing-places. Orion, 2001

This first sequel in the author's planned trilogy is on the same lines as the previous volume (E.1 above) but this time the Arthurian fantasy element is a good deal more prominent, taking up about half the content of a long, multi-chaptered book. Nevertheless the narrative of Arthur De Caldicot continues as a convincing picture of life in mediaeval England. The period covered is the nine months from January to October 1200, with King John struggling to maintain his authority and make preparations for a new Crusade going on throughout Europe.

Arthur begins to train as a squire in the service of Lord Stephen De Holt, who is planning to join the Crusade. During the spring and summer in England and France he learns about many practical matters, including horsemanship, weaponry, the threat from Wales beyond Offa's Dyke and marriage customs at all levels of society. At the same time he begins to think deeply about religion, with increasing awareness of the plight of the Jewish community in England and the growth of militant Christianity in France. The action of this realistic story depends hardly at all on the fantasy element.

Age range: 13 to 15

10. Hendry, Frances. Quest for a maid. Canongate, 1988.

Shortlisted for the Guardian Prize, this is a book with two contrasting aspects. The first, predominant in the opening and closing sections, takes the form of a romantic adventure story full of desperate escapades and often depending on very unlikely behaviour or even on supernatural powers. Alongside this is a carefully researched historical narrative centred on events in Scotland and Norway in the late thirteenth century. The author touches on Anglo-Scottish politics in featuring the struggle for supremacy between the Bruce family and its rivals after the death of King Alexander in 1286, but she does seem more interested in the social and domestic history of the period. Among topics set in context and highlighted are the management of a wealthy trader's household; the routines of a boat-builder's yard; the conduct of a witchcraft trial; and above all the drama of a battle against the elements in a doomed sea-voyage. All the contrasting scenes of high adventure and realism are seen through the eyes of Margaret Wright, aged only nine at the start, but always a dominant personality.

Age range: 11 to 14

11. Cushman, Karen. Catherine, called Birdy. Macmillan, 1994

This is a particular valuable historical story since it provides interesting characters and an increasing degree of tension while also offering a quite detailed account of everyday life in the late thirteenth century.

The novel takes the form of a diary begun by thirteen-year-old Catherine in September 1290, recounting her daily thoughts and experiences over the next twelve months. She lives on her father's small estate in Lincolnshire, enjoys the country life and the village festivals, but resents such things as the prevailing callousness towards animals, and is shocked to hear of the expulsion of the Jews from England. During the year her domineering father presses her to accept betrothal to an ageing Scots landowner known to her as Shaggy Beard. Her mother's difficult pregnancy is another terrible worry, but some of her family reveal unexpected strengths and at the last moment events take a turn in her favour. On one or two occasions the writing shifts briefly into extravagant farce but, in general, it is realism, whether stark or colourful, that predominates. After the ending there is a note by the American author which aims to put the story in historical context.

Age range: 11 to 14

PRIMARY SCHOOL LEVEL:

12. Platt, Richard. Castle diary: the journal of Tobias Burgess, page. Illuminated by Chris Riddell. Walker Books, 1999.

Tobias begins his diary in January,1285, as he is about the join his uncle's household as a page. As Tobias learns of his duties and castle life in the 13th century so we too are given many details both in the text and also in the wonderful illustrations which bring the words to life. Tobias not only studies fighting skills and learns to hunt, but explores the castle from top to bottom, full of curiosity about the kitchens and the garderobes. The year is full of special events like a tournament, harvest and Christmas. At the back of the book are several pages of notes about castle defences and warfare, social hierarchy and family life. The details of medieval weaponry are likely to fascinate anyone reading this book.

Tobias is full of life and very interested in everything going on. Through him we learn a great amount about life in an English castle during Plantagenet times and in a most enjoyable fashion too.

Age range: 8 to 11

13. Sutcliff, Rosemary. The witch's brat. Oxford U.P., 1970

The central character in this story from the early twelfth century is Lovel who, as an eleven-year-old disabled orphan, is driven from his village on suspicion of witchcraft. He finds refuge in a nearby abbey, and after showing some skill with herbal remedies is encouraged to train as a monk-physician. Later he moves to London where he becomes a monk at Smithfield and finds his vocation at the newly-built St. Bartholomew's Hospital. After the first chapters this is a quiet story of monastic life, much different from most of Sutcliff's longer novels. There are occasional references to major events of the period, such as the death of Henry I's son William when the White Ship foundered in 1120.

Age range: 8 to 11

14. Boston, Lucy. The stones of Green Knowe. Bodley Head, 1976

This story appeared as a late addition to the Green Knowe sequence and was intended as a finale, but it can perfectly well stand on its own as an example of the time-shift genre, set mainly in the early twelfth century. Roger d'Aulneaux is the eleven-year-old son of a Norman manorial lord, but one of his grandmothers is Saxon and the local smith who befriends him is of Viking descent. Roger is learning the skills of riding and hawking, and watching the erection of a new, stone-built hall, when he finds an ancient stone seat which can transport him forward in time. From Chapter 5 onwards the action shifts between the twelfth and later centuries, but the author seems primarily concerned to show how family life was developing in the earlier period. As in other parts of the sequence, the Norman hall, which becomes Green Knowe in the stories and Hemingford Grey in actual fact, is almost an additional character and certainly an essential link between the generations of people who have lived there in fiction and in reality. Illustrated by Peter Boston.

Age range: 8 to 11

Section F – British History 1300 to 1500

The later Middle Ages provide a rich variety of new themes for authors, and they clearly appealed strongly to Cynthia Harnett. Her novels were outstanding in the post-War decades and are still especially valuable to teachers for project work. More recently, Geraldine McCaughrean, Henrietta Branford and Terry Jones have written about the period in markedly contrasting styles.

Lead novels:

McCaughrean, G. A little lower than the angels, 1987. (Whitbread Award winner)
Harnett, C. The wool-pack, 1951 – reissued 2001. (Carnegie Medal winner)

Others at secondary school level:

Picard, B. Ransom for a knight, 1956
Picard, B. One is one, 1965
Welch, R. Bowman of Crecy, 1966
Sancha, S. Knight after Knight, 1991 (Revised version)
Branford, H. Fire, bed and bone, 1997. (Guardian Prize winner)
Harnett, C. Ring out, Bow Bells!, 1953
Harnett, C. The writing on the hearth, 1973.
Harnett, C. The load of unicorn, 1959.
Willard, E. The lark and the laurel, 1970. (Re-issued 1987)

Primary school level:

Welch, R. The gauntlet, 1951. (Reissued 1994)
Jones, T. The knight and the squire, with sequel. 1997/2000
Willard, E. The miller's boy, 1976. (Reissued 1989)

LEAD NOVELS:

1. McCaughrean, Geraldine. A little lower than the angels. Oxford U.P., 1987

In the late fourteenth century eleven-year-old Gabriel has been apprenticed to a brutal stonemason who maltreats him. He escapes by joining a troupe of Miracle Play performers and soon becomes one of their star actors. Inveigled into working faked miracles in the guise of an angel, he is tormented with guilt when he realises that the troupe's playmaster, Garvey, is an utter scoundrel who thrives on gullibility and fear. Matters come to a head when the players arrive at a deserted village and are pressed to perform by the local landowner. It turns out that the area has been devastated by plague and the sickly survivors are looking for a real miracle. Garvey departs and Gabriel is re-united with his parents, but decides to continue as a player in a reformed troupe.

This is a demanding book, optimistic at the end but presenting a fairly bleak picture of mediaeval peasant life and raising questions about innocence and exploitation. Readers could certainly learn a lot about the production of Miracle Plays, and about the mixed human motives of their producers.

Age range: 13 upwards

2. Harnett, Cynthia. The wool-pack. Methuen, 1951.

In 1493 Nicholas Fetterlock, teenage son of a prosperous Oxfordshire wool-merchant, is on the verge of adulthood. His father suggests betrothal to Cecily Bradshaw, the young daughter of a cloth-merchant, but the arrangements are put at risk by a mystery concerning shipments of wool to France and Italy. Nicholas and Cecily between them discover clues to a conspiracy and finally provide evidence which leads to the unmasking of the conspirators. The early chapters are mainly descriptive, but the thread of the plot is always kept in view until the action develops rapidly in the last five chapters.

The author's prime purpose is certainly to arouse interest

in the woollen and clothing industries of the fifteenth century and to weave into the story as much information as possible about sheep-farming and related matters. Other topics, such as the voyages of Columbus, the techniques of hawking or the new popularity of "golfe", are touched on with a light hand, so the book has obvious merit as an aid to history teaching. The author's own meticulous drawings are an added bonus. In a postscript to the text she lists some surviving Renaissance artefacts and suggests what to look for in museums.

Age range: 10 to 14

OTHERS AT SECONDARY SCHOOL LEVEL:

3. Picard, Barbara. Ransom for a knight. Oxford U.P., 1956

Barbara Picard was a prolific writer in the 1950s and 1960s who earned high praise for her re-tellings of traditional legends and also for two historical novels which were shortlisted for the Carnegie Medal. This one deals with the aftermath of the Scottish victory at Bannockburn in 1315. In the year following Alys de Renneville, aged twelve and living in Sussex, learns that her father and brother are being held for ransom near Perth. For credible reasons she sets off with a bag of jewels accompanied only by a boy-servant, and in almost a year of travelling makes her way through England and across the border to where the captives are held.

This is an enjoyable book with a strong story-line and a happy ending, but the author never hurries the action and is able to include a wealth of historical detail about town and country life in the early fourteenth century; York, for instance, then the second town of England, provides the background for one long chapter. A factual note following the last chapter refers to some problems of historical fiction writing, such as the difficulty of mixing real and invented characters. Illustrated by C. W. Hodges.

Age range: 11 to 14

4. Picard, Barbara. One is one. Oxford U.P., 1965

Also set in the fourteenth century, this time beginning in 1323, the central character is Stephen de Beauville, born into a knightly family, who, as a youth, is branded a coward and banished to a monastery. He runs away and proves his courage as a squire fighting in England and Scotland before returning to the monastery ten years later to develop his artistic interests. The author devotes much attention to the complexities of Stephen's character but she also finds space to portray the mediaeval society of the time in all its colourful variety. Her account of the monastic work of illuminating manuscripts, for instance, is exceptionally vivid. The illustrations are by Victor Ambrus.

Age range: 12 to 15

5. Welch, Ronald. Bowmen of Crecy. Oxford U.P., 1966

From a national point of view nothing in the fourteenth century was more important than the Hundred Years War, and one very obvious effect of the War throughout Britain was the constant demand for skilled archers. Ronald Welch, as an expert on military tactics and weaponry, is particularly well qualified to write against this background and, indeed, *Bowmen of Crecy* is up to his best standard. The central character is Hugh Fletcher who appears first as an outlaw defying authority on the Welsh borders, near Goodrich Castle. Like the legendary rebels of Sherwood Forest, Hugh and his followers are formidable archers but unlike Robin Hood he decides to give support to the King's armies against the French. The last section of the book covers the military operations leading up to the Battle of Crecy in 1346 and includes a quite detailed account of archery techniques and tactics. Welch never overuses his fund of knowledge, nor does be glorify war; Hugh has grown up in a violent society, but he finds the campaign in France "a dirty, sordid and brutal affair".

Age range: 11 to 14

6.Sancha, Sheila. Knight after knight. Walker, 1991.

Sancha is best known as a factual writer with an interest in early British history and architecture, but this venture into fiction writing is proof of her versatility. On the surface the story is no more than an amusing parody of the traditional mediaeval romance, featuring warring knights, damsels in distress and prisoners in dungeons. Many of the main characters are given suggestive names, such as Sir Payne Oldways or Sir Alexander Rich, and their behaviour is generally far removed from the realism of McCaughrean or Harnett. In the end the villains receive their just deserts and virtue is suitably rewarded.

Nevertheless, this is a book from which much may be learnt about life in England at the end of the fourteenth century. The author is a dedicated researcher and she shows excellent judgment in providing just enough detail from her knowledge of architecture, weaponry, costume, etc. The climactic siege of the villain's stronghold, for instance, is highly entertaining as well as informative while the course-by-course description of a celebration meal is truly memorable. The book is generously illustrated with the author's own small drawings but the text is quite sophisticated.

Age range: 10 to 14

7. Branford, Henrietta. Fire, bed and bone. Walker Books, 1997.

An unusual story seen through the eyes of a dog belonging to a poor village family at the time of the Peasant's Revolt. Rufus and Comfort, her owners, are sympathetic to the aims of the rebellion and are imprisoned not once but twice. After the second period of captivity Rufus is hanged, in spite of the promises of the king, who has agreed a pardon for all rebels.

The story is full of sights and smells important to a dog, and loyalty to the family does not stop her living rough at times, hunting the wild creatures of the woods. When the dog is living in the village, we get a vivid impression of the lifestyle endured by peasants during this time and the harsh conditions imposed by landowners which led to the uprising. We also hear tales of the battles and bloodshed which favour neither side. In this story the author succeeds in bringing vividly to life a rather neglected period of history.

Age range: 11 to 15

8. Harnett, Cynthia. Ring out, Bow Bells! Methuen, 1953.

As the title suggests, this novel is set in London in the early fifteenth century, when Sir Richard Whittington had been three times mayor. Whittington himself appears as a character and has a cat, but Ms Harnett suggests that the well-known legend was invented by him as a bedtime story. Most of the action concerns the doings of a group of apprentices, with many intriguing references to architectural features of which the author herself found surviving traces as she explored London in the 1940s and 1950s. In the last chapter she describes celebrations at the news of an English victory at Agincourt in 1415.

Age range: 10 to 14

9. Harnett, Cynthia. The writing on the hearth. Methuen, 1973.

Ms Harnett had the assistance of Gareth Lloyd as illustrator for this the last of her distinguished novels. It is not perhaps her liveliest work, but it still demonstrates her deep knowledge of the fifteenth century and her ability to re-create its characteristic features in a pleasantly readable way. The period this time is 1439-1441, with the Wars of the Roses not far away, and the setting is Ewelme in Oxfordshire. Fears of witchcraft and the complexities of heraldry are among the historical topics prominent in this story.

Age range: 10 to 14

10. Harnett, Cynthia. The load of unicorn. Methuen, 1959.

The 'load of Unicorn' of the title refers to a delivery of paper and the plot of this novel concerns the efforts of a group of scriveners to save their livelihoods from the threat of new technology: the printing press.

Caxton himself is a major character in the story, which centres around the London of St. Paul's and Westminster Abbey; Malory *(Morte d'Arthur)* also appears. London and pre-Shakespeare Stratford come to life as the adventure story unfolds; the plot contains much that is historically factually correct as it interweaves Lancastrian treason, customs evasion, early labour economies and family quarrels. Through the eyes of the hero, Bendy, the reader sees all too clearly the threats to the scribes as well as the excitement and risks of the new invention. The many illustrations and maps enhance and clarify elements of the text. Suitable for quite young children, and in its historical context very readable for anyone seeking an introduction to the late fifteenth century.

Age range: 9 to 14

11. Willard, Barbara. The lark and the laurel. Longman, 1970.

The first main story in the Mantlemass sequence (see Section G) is more of a romance than an historical story proper, especially in the closing chapters; there the teenage heroine Cecily Jolland falls passionately in love with Lewis Mallory and learns at last that she has already been betrothed to him as a young child. However, the earlier chapters which deal with the aftermath of Bosworth and the Wars of the Roses shed considerable light on the political and social history of the time. The author is deeply versed in the distant past of the old Sussex forest region whose people had a distinctive life-style and their own cherished traditions. She offers a convincing picture of the changing seasons, including Christmas festivities and a snow-bound Spring, and is also much concerned with the maltreatment of women by their men in the fifteenth century. The whole of the action takes place during eight or nine months in 1485/86.

Age range: 10 upwards

12. Welch, Ronald. The gauntlet. Oxford U.P., 1951

Most of Ronald Welch's books are clearly designed for young teenage readers, and all except this one are straightforward historical narratives. The gauntlet is a time-shift story with a child hero, and is intended for a younger age range. Its hero, Peter Staunton, is an English schoolboy with French connections. While staying with a friend in Wales he comes across a brass portrait of a Norman ancestor who had lived in the nearby Carreg Cennen Castle, and later, after handling a mysterious gauntlet, he finds himself back in the fourteenth century, transformed into the ancestor's son.

Life in the 1330s is uncomfortable and dangerous, but Peter adapts quickly and his experiences shed light on numerous aspects of mediaeval society. Eating arrangements, archery practice, falconry, heraldry and jousting are among the topics introduced and described in the author's usual fluent prose. In the closing chapters violence comes suddenly to the castle when a Welsh army besieges it, and Peter performs valiantly before re-awakening in the twentieth century. Time-shift stories were quite rare in the 1950s, but this is a good example of how they can serve to arouse interest in the distant past.

Age range: 9 to 13

13. Jones, Terry. The knight and the squire. Pavilion, 1997

The year is 1359, and young Tom, having acquired some priestly learning n his backwater English village, runs away from home with high hopes of military glory overseas. With the help of another runaway, known as Alan, he enters the service of a rascally knight. The realities of the Hundred Years War in Europe provide swift disillusionment for Tom. He and Alan are thrust into a series of desperate escapades, sometimes ludicrous or verging on fantasy, but also involving all kinds of brutality and pillage. In one particularly vivid scene Tom witnesses the wanton burning of a monastic library, with centuries of learning sacrificed to create a brief diversion. In the closing chapters Alan is revealed to be a girl and some historical figures like the Black Prince appear as characters.

This is an unusual story in that the author writes for a younger audience and generally uses a light-hearted tone with ample doses of comedy. He includes plenty of background detail, sometimes addressing the reader directly, and is at pains to show the utter confusion of mediaeval war and the dubious motives of its leaders. With 284 pages this is a longish book, but Michael Foreman's illustrations are no doubt helpful.

14. A sequel, *The lady and the squire* **(Pavilion 2000) has been published.**

Age range: 9 to 12

15. Willard, Barbara. The miller's boy. Penguin, 1976

In 1478 Thomas Welfare, aged eleven, is a reluctant labourer in his grandfather's mill in Sussex. As the seasons progress he mingles adult work with youthful pursuits and develops a close, but ultimately impossible, friendship with Lewis Mallory, ward and kinsman of a local landowner. After the mill has collapsed in a storm Thomas decides to leave the area and seek his fortune elsewhere. Primarily the story of a friendship, but also providing many sidelights on life in pre-Tudor England, with some emphasis on the vital role of horses in a rural society. Several characters from *The lark and the laurel* (See No.11, above) appear in this story, which could serve as an introduction to the Mantlemass series.

Age range: 9 to 12

SECTION G: BRITISH HISTORY, 1500 – 1600

The Tudor period has all the glamour and excitement that novelists could wish for but, as it happens among notable children's writers, only Barbara Willard in the 1970s has set out to make full use of it. However, more recently Susan Cooper and Susan Price have both chosen the period for large sections of their successful time-switch novels for older readers.

Lead novels:

Cooper, S. King of Shadows, 1999. (Carnegie Medal and Guardian Award shortlisted).
Willard, B. The sprig of broom, 1972. (Guardian Award shortlisted).

Others at secondary school level:

Willard, B. A cold wind blowing, 1972.
Willard, B. The iron lily, 1973. (Guardian Award winner: also two others in the series).
Harnett, C. Stars of Fortune, 1956
Hendry, F. Quest for a queen, 1989 – 93 (3 volumes).
Trease, G. Cloak for a spy, 1996.
Hunter, M. The Spanish letters, 1964.
Hunter, M. The thirteenth member, 1971.
Forest, A. The player's boy, 1970, with sequel.
Price, S. The Sterkarm handshake, 1998
Welch, R. The hawk, 1967.

Primary school level:

Prince, A. My Tudor queen, 2001.
Sutcliff, R. The armourer's house, 1951.
Sutcliff, R. The Queen Elizabeth story, 1950.

LEAD NOVELS:

1. Cooper, Susan. King of Shadows. Bodley Head, 1999.

In the summer of 1999 young teenager Nathan Field comes to London from America to join a boys' theatre group preparing for a production of *A midsummer night's dream* at the re-built Globe Theatre. After feeling ill during a rehearsal he goes to bed with a high fever and wakes up next morning four hundred years earlier in the comfortless London of 1599. He finds himself with his twentieth century mind in the body of another Nat Field, cast as Puck in an early production of the same play at the original Globe Theatre.

With his American accent seeming quite normal for the time, Nat soon learns to cope with Elizabethan living conditions. The rough clothing, the monotonous food washed down with frequent draughts of thin ale, the glamour and chaos of the streets are all bearable; but the savagery of the bear-pit and the sadistic glee of its devotees are altogether too much for him. At rehearsals he adapts well to the arduous practice of the time and soon meets Shakespeare himself in the role of Oberon. Queen Elizabeth and Robert Cecil also appear briefly before Nat wakes up again in a modern hospital. In this time-switch story nearly two-thirds of the action and all the liveliest characters belong to the historical sections. There is a brief theatrical bibliography at the end.

Age range: 10 to 14.

2. Willard, Barbara. The sprig of broom, Longman, 1971.

One of the Mantlemass series, this story begins in 1506 and tells of Medley Plashet, a boy with secrets to solve. His father has a mysterious past and abandons Medley and his mother when strange men track him down. One of them, Kit Crispin, befriends Medley and promises to help him. As a pledge Kit gives him a sprig of broom to plant, the symbol of the Plantaganet dynasty. Medley falls in love with Catherine, the daughter of the lord of Mantlemass, but he has no proper name, no money, and no idea if his father's secret is an honourable one or not. To achieve happiness and his heart's desire he has to seek him out.

A compulsive tale, speculating on what might have happened to a son of Richard III who had decided to live in obscurity, rather than contest the throne, after the Battle of Bosworth. The author claims that a builder and craftsman called Richard Plantaganet did indeed live in Kent until 1550. What he did between 1485 and his death is open to speculation but there may be more than a grain of truth in this account. In any case, the story is well worth reading as a literary experience and for general historical interest.

Age range: 10 upwards.

3. Willard, Barbara. A cold wind blowing, Longman, 1972.

This story demonstrates how political events, seemingly of little relevance to country folk living far from London and the life at Court, can have devastating effects when the consequences reach them.

Piers honours a promise made to his uncle to go to his aid when the destruction of the monasteries reaches his Priory, and finds himself encumbered with a strange girl. Only a promise made to his dying uncle makes him bring the girl back to the safety of his home. At first silent and strange, the girl gradually sheds her secrets and, for a few months, Piers and Isabella are happy, married and with a child on the way. However tragedy finally catches up with them and Piers is left grieving.

The dissolution of the monasteries by Henry VIII is shown to have very real consequences in this story for everyday men and women, taking some of them to the scaffold and others to imprisonment. A powerful story, which is overshadowed with impending doom from the first.

Age range: 12 to 15.

4. Willard, Barbara. The iron lily. Longman, 1973.

This is the story of Lilias Godman, a widow, who sets herself up as the master of an iron foundry in the forests near Mantlemass. She also has a secret to unravel about her past and specifically her parentage. A clue is revealed to her after her mother's death – the name Medley – and she resolves to discover the truth about her links with the Mantlemass family. She is a hard woman and sticks to her plans tenaciously, nearly ruining her daughter's happiness in the process, but in the end she achieves some measure of happiness.

An offshoot of the Mantlemass dynasty, this story is set in the time of Elizabeth I with the beginnings of industrial development taking its place alongside the rural forest life. Protestantism is still in its infancy and any hint of a leaning towards Catholicism is dangerous. In addition a looming shadow is cast over everything – the fear of a Spanish invasion.

Age range: 12 to 15.

5. Willard, Barbara. The eldest son. Kestral, 1977.
6. Willard, Barbara. Flight of swans. Kestral, 1980.

These two later additions to the Mantlemass series are both set in the sixteenth century, the former in the reign of Henry VIII and the latter in the Elizabethan period, starting in 1585.

Age range: 12 to 15

7. Harnett, Cynthia. Stars of fortune. Methuen, 1956.

The date for this story is 1554, the year after Wyatt's Rebellion, with the future Queen Elizabeth under house arrest at Woodstock. The child characters are members of the actual Washington family of Sulgrave Manor, from which George Washington later emerged as the American hero. The plot is concerned with the quandary of those who supported Elizabeth in principle but were reluctant to risk their lives and property through rash involvement in the schemes of hot-heads. The imagined secret visit of Elizabeth to consult a fortune-teller at Sulgrave makes a good story and is as usual well supported by the author's own detailed illustrations. Ms Harnett is as much at home in the sixteenth century as in the fifteenth – see four entries in section F, above.

Age range: 10 to 14.

8. a, b, c. Hendry, Frances. Quest for a queen; a. The falcon. b. The lark. c. The jackdaw. Canongate, 1989, 1992 and 1993.

These three novels are closely linked and together amount to a lengthy chronicle, of some 750 pages, covering the period from 1565 to 1587. The Queen in question is, of course, Mary Queen of Scots, who appears in the first story soon after her marriage to Darnley in 1565. She is the central historical figure in all three novels, especially the first, in which Darnley, Bothwell, Rizzio and John Knox also feature prominently. In the third story, set mainly in London, Anthony Babington of the Babington Plot appears almost throughout, as does the spymaster Walsingham; Queen Elizabeth is in the background, appearing personally in one later chapter. The author aims at a degree of impartiality in presenting these real personalities, though her sympathies are clearly with the Scottish Queen, and her contempt for John Knox is made very plain indeed. Her research into sixteenth century politics in Scotland and England appears to have been thorough.

Each story also has a cast of invented characters, many of them adults engaged in sexual intrigues, or, in the case of the males, brutal and abusive in the extreme. For the most part vice and virtue are suitably rewarded in the end, but the author has no interest in glamourizing Elizabethan society nor in glossing over its injustices. These are clearly novels for teenagers with reading stamina, much more sophisticated than some others from this author.

Age range: 14 upwards.

9. Trease, Geoffrey. Cloak for a spy. Macmillan, 1997

For his very last book Geoffrey returned to the Elizabethan period which had served him as a background for several novels written during the previous fifty or sixty years, including the well-known *Cue for Treason,* 1940. This new story is set in the 1580s, just before the Spanish Armada. Travelling on the continent with a supposed tutor – actually a spy of Walsingham's – teenager Giles Taberdar gets involved in the search for secret Armada plans and runs into acute danger. Thanks to the support of a spirited Italian girl , Giles and the tutor escape from Spanish counter-spies and return to England with vital information for Walsingham. The last chapter touches briefly on preparations for national defence, including Queen Elizabeth's famous speech at Tilbury, and on the outcome of the Armada.

In all his historical novels Trease aims to strike a balance between entertainment and instruction. The balance is about right here, though the didactic element is strong throughout, with most of the excitement reserved for the closing chapters.

Age range: 11 to 14.

10. Hunter, Mollie. The Spanish letters. Evans, 1964.

Jamie Morton is a "caddie", or visitor's guide to the streets of Edinburgh, aged fifteen when the story begins in 1589. His life changes drastically when he agrees to work for Robert Macey, an Englishman sent from London to counter the dangerous activities of Spanish plotters against the thrones of England and Scotland . Like many of Ms Hunter's young heroes, Jamie employs an effective if not always scrupulous mixture of courage and cunning to achieve his ends and is suitably rewarded.. The central plot is pretty much of the blood-and-thunder variety, with one desperate adventure following another and a variety of colourful villains headed by the Spaniard, D'Aquirre. At the same time, the author is obviously well-versed in the political complexities of the time and gives the reader every chance to develop an interest in Scottish affairs on the verge of the union with England. There is no excessive sentiment or ranting nationalism in this story.

Age range: 12 to 15.

11.Hunter, Mollie. The thirteenth member. Hamilton. 1971.

In late sixteenth century Scotland Gilly Duncan, aged fifteen, is the reluctant thirteenth member of a witches' coven whose members practice satanic rituals and attempt to work black magic. She is befriended by Adam Gowrie, a pauper child of hanged parents, and Gideon Grahame, a scholarly alchemist. Between them they foil a plot to contrive the death of the Scottish king, afterwards James I in England, and are able to plead their case to the king himself at Holyrood Palace. The king's unpredictable behaviour reflects his famously strange character – intelligent, sometimes irrational but disposed to be merciful. In this action-packed story most of the witches and warlocks are no innocents but rather evil-doers who, by the standards of a brutal age, get their just deserts under the anti-witchcraft laws.

Age range: 14 to 16.

12.Forest, Antonia. The player's boy. Faber, 1970.

Ms Forest is best known for her ten-volume sequence of novels about the Marlow family in the 1940s, two of which were on Carnegie Medal shortlists, but here she creates a supposed ancestor of the Marlows in the late Tudor period. Nicholas Marlow runs away from an unhappy home and school at the age of eleven in 1593 to serve briefly as ship's boy and then as a theatre apprentice in London. He meets his namesake Christopher Marlowe, afterwards murdered, and works for five years in Shakespeare's company, where genius is at work and theatrical history in the making. Through his experience the reader learns much about the religious and political conflicts of the time, resulting often in the torture of prisoners and public executions. A sequel (13. *The players and the rebels,* Faber, 1971) deals with the impact of the Essex rebellion on the players. Both novels are most likely to be enjoyed by readers with previous knowledge of the Elizabethan theatre or a developing interest in it.

Age range: 12 to 15

14. Price, Susan. The Sterkarm handshake,. Scholastic,1998.

Whilst this is not a historical account as such, and involves a certain amount of fantasy in the imagination of a "Time Tube" which links the 21st century with the 16th, the scientist who uses the Tube and lives with the Sterkarm clan is there to observe their lifestyle; through her detailed notes we can learn a lot about rural life of the period. The educational content is absorbed as we read the gripping story and wonder which way Andrea will turn, torn between her modern lifestyle and her love for a 16th century chieftain's son. The clash between the cultures separated by centuries is fascinating, and disaster looms from the first.

This portrayal of the borderland with clan raids and difficult living conditions gives a valuable insight into a part of the country and a time period not covered by many other writers. Whilst life there may have been hard, there are positive aspects, such as the cleaner environment and the value placed on individuals in the communal living system, which the 21st century is demonstrated to have lost.

Age range: 13 to 15

15. Welch, Ronald. The hawk. Oxford University Press, 1967.

In chronological sequence this is the next Carey story after *Knight Crusader* (see Section E, No. 5) and is set in the early 1580s. The central character, Harry Carey, is primarily a seaman engaged in the pre-Armada hostilities between England and Spain. In the later chapters he comes ashore to work for the spymaster Walsingham and has a share in the exposure of the Babington conspiracy in 1584.

Age range: 11 to 14.

PRIMARY SCHOOL LEVEL:

16.Prince, Alison. My Tudor queen. Scholastic, 2001.

This book belongs to a diary-form series which has an obvious aim of illuminating certain events or important periods in British history. However, in the hands of a prize-winning author it becomes something rather better than an easy-reading history unit. Ms Prince's diarist is Eva de Puebla, a lady-in-waiting to Catherine of Aragon, who comes to London with the Spanish party in 1501. Through Eva's eyes we see the complicated series of events which included Catherine's marriages first to Prince Arthur and, after his death, to Henry VIII, finishing soon after the Battle of Flodden in 1513. Brief factual notes and illustrations at the end of the book provide further background information about the period.

All the main characters in this story are drawn from history with Catherine and Henry cast in leading roles and shown with their known strengths and weaknesses. The author is particularly concerned to show how women and children are routinely victimized by their Tudor men, and how the course of European history was often determined by personality clashes and individual follies.

Age range: 9 to 12

17.Sutcliff, Rosemary. The armourer's house. Oxford University Press, 1951.

Before she made her reputation with a complex series of novels set in early Britain, Ms Sutcliff wrote several simple but frequently re-issued stories in the Tudor period. This one is set in the reign of Henry VIII, probably c. 1535, and covers a year in the life of nine year old Tamsyn Caunter, who moves from her childhood home in Devonshire to stay with her uncle in London. The uncle is a skilled amourer, but Tamsyn has grown up with an intense love of sailing-ships, and the highlight of her year is a visit to the Royal Dockyard at Deptford. There she and the reader learn something of the techniques of Tudor shipbuilding and have a glimpse of Henry's famous warship at the Mary Rose. Tamsyn sees nothing of the darker side of London life at the time, but she does catch sight of Henry and his doomed wife Anne Boleyn, looking ominously unhappy. The story ends up with a family reunion at Christmas and is perhaps over-sentimental by current standards, but shows much of the author's familiar skill in describing simple pleasures. Illustrated by C. W. Hodges.

Age range: 8 to 11.

18.Sutcliff, Rosemary. The Queen Elizabeth story. Oxford University Press, 1950.

A year in the life of Perdita Pettle, aged eight at the start, who lives with her parents and elder bother in a rectory near Bideford in Devon. The date is quite early in Elizabeth's reign, probably 1669/70. Through Perdita's eyes the reader sees many aspects of rural life at the time, such as a summer fair in Bideford and the celebrations of Christmas at the rectory; the family are not especially wealthy but they enjoy special festive food , elaborate decorations and a visit from the local mummers on Christmas Eve. The climax occurs in June of the following summer when the Queen herself makes a state visit to Devon. Perdita is chosen to make a presentation, is disappointed through illness, but finally meets the royal visitor in person. The detailed illustrations by C. W. Hodges include a particularly memorable drawing of a sailing-ship ready to leave the quayside at Bideford.

Age range: 8 to 11

Section H British History, 1600 – 1750

In the era of the Stuarts and the English Civil War writers are obliged to consider the merits of impartiality in areas which even today can arouse strong feelings in some of their readers. Rosemary Sutcliff, writing outside her preferred pre-Tudor periods, is one who possesses a sure touch, while Jamila Gavin for older children and Lucy Boston for pre-teenagers are among those capturing the atmosphere of the times with their very different methods.

Lead novel:

Gavin, J. Coram boy, 2000 (Whitbread Award winner).

Others at secondary school level:

Sutcliff, R Simon, 1953.
Willard, B. Harrow and harvest, 1974, and The keys of Mantlemass, 1981.
Westall, R. The devil on the road, 1978 (Carnegie Medal shortlisted).
Rees, C. Witch girl, 2000.
Walsh, J. P. A parcel of patterns, 1983.
Willard, B. Ned only, 1985.
Trease, G. Popinjay Stairs, 1973.
Sutcliff, R. Bonnie Dundee, 1983.
McCaughrean, G. Plundering paradise, 1996.
Hunter, M. The Lothian run, 1971.
Hendry, F. Quest for a kelpie, 1986.
Welch, R. For the king, 1961.
Welch, R. Captain of Dragoons, 1956.

Primary school level:

Boston, L. The children of Green Knowe, 1954 (Carnegie Medal shortlisted).
Doherty, B. Children of winter, 1985.

LEAD NOVEL:

1.Gavin, Jamila. Coram boy. Mammoth, 2000.

The first part of this long, emotional and often quite horrifying novel begins in the year of 1741. An early character is Otis Gardiner, ostensibly concerned with the welfare of unwanted babies but actually a sadistic killer. Soon the scene shifts to a choir-school in Gloucester, where teenager Alexander Ashbrook is a pupil, and then to the luxurious Ashbrook House. Alexander defies his wealthy parents in determining to make his career in music, and leaves home after unknowingly fathering a child. Part 2 of the novel, beginning eight years later, is centred in Coram House, a refuge for homeless children, where Alexander's child Aaron is growing up in friendship with a black boy, Toby. Characters from Part 1, including the villainous Otis, now a Coram benefactor, re-appear at intervals, and as one revelation follows another the story moves towards a rather melodramatic climax.

The author's main purpose throughout is to highlight the soul-destroying and brutalizing effects of poverty in the eighteenth century and, in particular, the plight of unwanted children. At a subsidiary level she makes a case for the nurturing of musical talent and its power to transform lives; in Part 2 the composer Handel and musicologist Charles Burney appear as influential characters.

Age range: 14 upwards.

OTHERS AT SECONDARY SCHOOL LEVEL:

2.Sutcliff, Rosemary. Simon, Oxford U. P., 1953.

Chapter 1 introduces Simon and Amias, two Cornish schoolboys aged about eleven who in 1640 can be friends in spite of their families' differing political views. After the outbreak of the Civil War friendship becomes difficult as Simon supports the Roundheads, and within five years he has joined the New Model Army to fight at the Battle of Naseby. Though life in Cornwall continues much as normal between outbreaks of violence, Simon and Amias continue to fight on opposite sides until the defeat of the

Royalists and the execution of the King. Peace returns to Cornwall in 1649 and the two young men are able to resume their friendship.

The Civil war is seen mainly through the eyes of Simon and so the Roundheads, and especially General Fairfax, appear in quite a favourable light. Fanaticism is strikingly represented in the Roundhead soldier known as Zeal-of-the-Lord. In a brief historical note the author expresses her determination to present the facts of the fighting in Cornwall as accurately as possible, and to avoid bias in dealing with controversial incidents at the Battle of Torrington.

Age range: 11 to 14.

3.Willard, Barbara. Harrow and harvest. Kestrel, 1974.

This last volume in the main Mantlemass sequence, set in the middle period of the English Civil War from about November 1642 to August 1644, is a powerful piece of writing but essentially tragic. The families connected with Mantlemass are utterly disunited divided not only by different feelings about the War but also by personal feuds and long-standing grievances. Although national conflict provides a constant background and crucial events such as the Battle of Marston Moor are reported, the emphasis here is decidedly on family matters and the affairs of the community around Mantlemass. The ending is somber indeed as most of the few survivors decide to leave England in search of a new life in America.

4.A supplementary volume, The keys of Mantlemass (Kestrel 1981), consists of a group of episodes ranging over the period 1485 to 1644 and also includes a story about some American descendants who visit Sussex 300 years later.

Age range: 12 to 15.

5.Westall, Robert. The devil on the road. Macmillan, 1978.

Westall is perhaps best known for his realistic narratives

of Britain in the 1940s but his large output also included ghost stories of all kinds, often suggesting the malign influence of past events. *The devil on the road,* which was shortlisted for the Carnegie Medal, is in this category but is unusual both for its Suffolk setting and for its featuring of a well-known historical episode, the East Anglian witch-hunting hysteria of the 1640s. Away from his native Tyneside, Westall may not be too convincing in the build-up and conclusion of this time-shift story; but when his narrator John Webster finds himself among the Puritan hunters and their victims the writing becomes vivid and passionate. In a note at the end of the book Westall refers to the history of witch-hunting and its modern parallels.

Age range: 14 upwards.

6.Rees, Celia. Witch Child. Bloomsbury, 2000.

Mary Newbury's supposed journal begins in 1659 when her grandmother is put to death for witchcraft in the course of a witch-hunting frenzy. Mary is herself suspected but is helped to join a party of Puritan emigrants on their way to the New World. The first sections of the book, about a third of the whole, have a strictly factual background of peasant life in England at the end of the Cromwellian period and of the perils of an Atlantic crossing. The emigrants' experiences as pioneers in America are described in equally vivid terms but the author loses some credibility by hinting that real witchcraft is afoot. Ms Rees became known in the 1990s as a writer of teenage thrillers, sometimes rather lurid and with supernatural elements. This one just about qualifies as a genuine historical novel and was shortlisted for the Guardian Prize.

Age range: 12 to 15.

7.Walsh, Jill Paton. A Parcel of Patterns. Kestrel, 1983.

The narrator of this starkly realistic story is Moll Percival a teenage girl who has supposedly survived the outbreak of plague in Eyam, who decides to write an account of it before emigrating to America. Her story begins in the mid 1650s when, as a young child, she had met Thomas Torre who became her devoted admirer. Moll paints a vivid picture of life in Derbyshire in the post-Restoration years with the contrast between Puritanism and joie-de-vivre personified in the characters of the old clergyman Mr. Stanley and his young successor Mr. Mompellion. When the plague arrives and claims one victim after another, the clergymen sink their differences to rally the despairing villagers.

The author opts for complete frankness and honesty in describing the effects of a lethal epidemic on a community which had to rely on folk-lore medicine and primitive hygiene. Records show that less than a hundred people from Eyam's population of about 350 were alive when the plague died out in the autumn of 1666. Moll's account covers the illness and death of most of her family and friends with harrowing references to the disposal of bodies.

Age range: 14 upwards.

8. Willard, Barbara. Ned Only. MacRae, 1985.

Young teenager Ned is the despised kitchen-boy in the household of Sir Joshua Bidgood, a 'nouveau riche' Sussex landowner of the 1660s. The first half of *Ned Only* is an upstairs/downstairs story in Willard's familiar Mantlemass vein, pointing a stark contrast between the comfortable life of a landowning family and the miserable existence of their servants. Ned's fortunes take a turn for the better through the influence of the highly-principled Mr. Ransom, tutor for Sir Joshua's son, but for some time Sir Joshua himself continues as a brutal dictator at Winterpicks Manor.

There is a sudden change about halfway through the novel, when a palace revolution occurs and Ned shares in desperate adventures in the forests and byways of Sussex and Kent. One sensation follows another until Ned and his friends gain their hearts' desires and Sir Joshua is utterly confounded. This sort of near-melodrama is very different from the Mantlemass style and is perhaps more likely to hold the attention of the average young reader. The historical background remains impeccable, with late

references to the Fire of London and some particularly vivid
glimpses of Welsh drovers sweeping all before them.

Age range: 11 to 14.

9.Trease, Geoffrey. Popinjay Stairs. Macmillan, 1973.

The scene is set in the London of 1673. The main
fictional characters are Denzil Swift, an off-duty junior naval officer,
and Deborah Fane, a spirited young woman who writes plays
under a male pseudonym. After involvement in a highway robbery
they join forces with a character from history - Samuel Pepys, the
diarist and Admiralty official. Pepys enters the plot when secret
documents are stolen, with his reputation threatened and
England's security at stake. The action moves at a great pace
through London's dangerous streets and its fashionable theatre-
land, finishing with a riverside rescue and a perilous chase down
the Thames.

Although the novel could be read as a pacy adventure
story, Trease loses no opportunity to link the action with
Restoration politics and society. Pepys in his later years is drawn
from life, while there are passing references to events like the Fire
of London or the Medway naval disgrace, and to fashionable habits
such as the wearing of spectacular clothes or the urge to unravel
scientific mysteries. Deborah is a credible early feminist, much
frustrated by the conventions of the age.

Age range: 11 to 14.

10.Sutcliff, Rosemary. Bonnie Dundee. Bodley Head, 1983.

The narrator is Hugh Herriott, a Scottish exile in Holland,
who recounts the story of his adventurous youth starting at the age
of thirteen in 1682. At that date Charles II was near the end of his
reign and Scotland was in a state of turmoil. Herriott tells of his
involvement with John Graham of Claverhouse, also known as
Bonnie Dundee, who appears as a leading character up to his death
at Killiecrankie in 1689, and with other Covenanters and the early

Jacobites in Scotland. Other events featured in the narrative are from English history such as the Ryehouse Plot and the Monmouth Rebellion. The closing chapters cover James II's defeat in Ireland and the narrator's service in the French army.

Ms. Sutcliff as usual tells an excellent story with fine descriptive passages and is scrupulously fair to all parties. However the background of historical fact is much more prominent than in the Roman novels and could be confusing to those without previous knowledge of the period. In school it might serve as a follow-up to some study of the seventeenth century.

Age range: 11 to 14.

11.McCaughrean, Geraldine. Plundering paradise. Oxford U.P., 1996.

In 1717 Nathan Gull, aged fourteen, is at boarding school when he learns that his clergyman father has died penniless. Despised by the headmaster and most of the pupils, Nathan is befriended by Tamo White, son of a rich piratical seaman, now deceased, and a Madagascan mother. Tamo is about to leave for Madagascar and invites Nathan and his younger sister Maud to join the party. Paradise seems to be in prospect, but their ship turns out to be a slave-trader with a villainous captain. The children escape to a remote village where for two years they struggle to survive, beset by natural hazards, village practices and English pirate raids. In the end their luck turns and Nathan returns to England with ample funds; Maud however decides to stay with Tamo and the natives.

This is a rollicking adventure story told with the author's usual irreverent zest, but the characters are well-drawn and the period detail is, no doubt, accurate enough. Readers are invited to compare the supposedly advanced civilization of slave-trading Europe with the superstitious but relatively peaceful life-style of the Madagascan village community.

Age range: 12 to 15.

12.Hunter, Mollie. The Lothian run. Hamilton, 1971.

In 1736 Sandy Maxwell, aged sixteen and increasingly restless, is apprenticed to a staid Edinburgh lawyer. A chance meeting with a mysterious government investigator brings him all the excitement he could wish for, as he learns of deadly secrets and is involved both with the smugglers of the Lothian run and with Jacobite agents such as the ruthless mercenary Kevin St. Clair. Amid mounting tension the action shifts between town and country, culminating in a graphic description of the Porteous Riots of September 1736, when an Edinburgh mob did, in fact, storm the Tolbooth Jail.

Edinburgh in the 1730s had a veneer of peaceful progress, while beneath the surface the threat of Jacobite rebellion was only too real. Ms. Hunter is no romantic about the Jacobites. In the person of Mr. Ogilvie, a devout priest, she represents the idealism and loyalty which sustained the rebels, but he appears a mere pawn in the hands of St. Clair and other ruffians who fomented rebellion for their own reasons. Her young hero is a convincing creation, brave without much political awareness and ready to support whatever faction is the first to offer him the chance of adventure.

Age range: 12 to 15.

13.Hendry, Frances. Quest for a kelpie. Canongate, 1986.

On her seventieth birthday Jeannie Gillies looks back to her early years growing up in north-east Scotland, at the time of the 1745 Jacobite rebellion. She describes her life firstly as a nine-year-old girl, helping her family to eke out a precarious living in a remote fishing community, and then as a servant in the household of a doctor in Nairn. Most of the people there are too busy with their own problems to care much about the rebellion, but all are involved when first the Highlanders and soon afterwards the King's army are quartered in Nairn. Loyalties are divided, with the local people victimized by both sides. Jeannie, now thirteen, is torn between conflicting feelings, and is forced to search her conscience before the Battle of Culloden.

Several of the characters are drawn from historical records, while both the social and political backgrounds are convincingly built up behind a fast-moving, all-action story. The climax involves the fulfilment of a gypsy prophecy, but supernatural matters are kept within bounds and the still-controversial events of the time are presented with scrupulous fairness.

Age range: 11 to 14.

14. Welch, Ronald.   For the King. Oxford U.P., 1961.
15. Captain of Dragoons. Oxford U.P., 1956.

In these two stories Welch continues the adventures of the Carey family. In the first he places Neil Carey on the Royalist side in the Civil War, 1641 - 45, but is careful to present a balanced picture of the conflict and shows the fanatics of both sides in an unfavourable light. In the second, the central character is Charles Carey, who fights with Marlborough in the campaigns leading up to Blenheim, 1704. He also serves as a secret agent in France where the Jacobite rebels are hatching their plots around the Old Pretender.

Age range: 11 to 14.

PRIMARY SCHOOL LEVEL:

16. Boston, Lucy. The children of Green Knowe. Faber, 1954.

Although not so obviously relevant to historical studies as the last in the Green Knowe sequence (see section E, No. 14), this opening volume was inspired by the author's consuming interest in the passage of time and has the power to make others share her passion. Seven-year-old Tolly Oldknow comes to stay with his great-grandmother in her ancestral home and listens to her stories about its past occupants, especially the three children who lived there in the mid-seventeenth century. Toby, Alexander and Linnet each have stories of their own concerned for the most part with memorable domestic incidents - although Charles II as a patron of music does appear briefly in Alexander's story.

Apart from these sub-narratives, there is a time-shift element in the book since Tolly manages to imagine his way back into the seventeenth century and joins the three children in the garden of Green Knowe. However there is none of the rather clumsy changeover machinery found in some time-switch stories; here the transition from present to past and back again is barely noticeable. Green Knowe with its colourful past is indeed a notable literary creation, while for younger readers Peter Boston's detailed illustrations provide an added bonus.

Age range: 6 to 10.

17.Doherty, Berlie. Children of winter. Methuen, 1985.

This is another time-switch story featuring the later seventeenth century, but Berlie Doherty is a conventional and down-to-earth writer by comparison with Lucy Boston. Her three modern children take refuge from stormy weather in an old Derbyshire barn and find themselves transported back to an age when whole communities could be devastated by plague, as at Eyam a few years before. The children in their earlier incarnation have to live through a whole winter in isolation, struggling to survive and desperate for news of their relatives in the nearby village. Obviously this situation is not exactly typical of the time but readers are encouraged to empathize with the children and gain some insight into their attitudes and problems.

Age range: 8 to 12.

APPENDIX 1.

Children's Book Awards

In Britain there are three prestigious annual awards which are mainly concerned with newly-published fiction:

1.Carnegie Medal: 1936 onwards.
2.The Guardian Award: 1966 -
3.Whitbread Award: 1972 -

The Carnegie judges gave ample encouragement to historical writing between 1950 and 1975, but since then have shown only occasional interest. In recent decades both the Guardian and the Whitbread panels have selected a good range of historical novels for all periods.

Other current British awards include the Smarties Prize (1985 -), which caters for age-ranges up to eleven, and the Kurt Maschler, which aims to reward the best combinations of text with illustration. Other relevant awards, no longer current, have been sponsored in recent years by the Observer (1981 - 1987); the Children's Rights Workshop (1974 - 1987); and the Writers' Guild (1991 - 1997). There are also separate awards in Scotland, Wales and Ireland.

In the United States the prime award is the Newbery Medal. Since 1922 the Newbery judges have regularly shown an interest in historical writing, including British history on several occasions. Among many other American awards the Phoenix (1985 -) is unusual; its judges consider undervalued books published twenty years previously. Their first choice, for the year 1965, was Rosemary Sutcliff's *The mark of the horse lord* and they have since nominated several other novels relating to more recent British history.

APPENDIX 2.

Short stories.

1. Cooling, Wendy. Centuries of stories. Harper/Collins, 1999. To celebrate the millennium, Wendy Cooling persuaded twenty current authors of note to contribute to this collection which has one story for each century A.D. since the first. Most of the authors are not specialists in history, however, and few are as successful as Robert Swindells with his fifth-century post-Roman story. Several contributors did append historical notes to their stories but, without a linking framework, the collection seems to be of limited value.

2 .McCaughrean, Geraldine. Britannia; 100 great stories from British history. Orion, 1998.These brief narratives are intended f or younger readers and reflect the author's wide literary experience and genuine interest in history, but they come on the borderline between fact and fiction. They are now being re-issued in five separate paperbacks.

3. Streatfield, Noel. The fearless treasure. Joseph, 1953. Writing nearly fifty years before Ms. McCaughrean, Ms. Streatfield devised an ingenious framework to enable her imaginary group of schoolchildren to gain some awareness of British history in general and of eight periods of history in particular, starting in 43 A.D. Ms. Streatfield was a gifted writer whose best work has stood the test of time, but her tone here is perhaps rather too earnest and didactic and this book will not be found in many libraries nowadays.

4. Since 1995 a series of shortish historical novels called Flashbacks have been appearing from the publishers A. & C. Black. As with all such series the quality is variable, but among the prize-winning authors contributing are Adele Geras, Theresa Breslin, Susan Price and Melvin Burgess.

INDEX OF AUTHORS

The reference given after each name is to the lettered Section in the text and the number within each Section.

Sancha, S.	F6				
Speare, E.	C8				
Sutcliff, R.	A1	A6	A7	B15	C2	C3
	C4	C5	C6	C11	D1	D2
	E3	E4	E13	G17	G18	H2
	H10				
Swindells, R.	A4				
Tomlinson, T.	E6	E7	E8		
Trease, G.	B10	B14	C9	G9	H9
Treece, H.	A5	B13	C7	C10	D6a
	D6b	D6c	D11		
Turnbull, A.	B11				
Walsh, J.P.	H7				
Welch, R.	E5	F5	F12	G15	H14
	H15				
Westall, R.	H5				
Willard, B.	F11	F15	G2	G3	G4	G5
	G6	H3	H4	H8		

INDEX OF TITLES

The reference given after each title is to the lettered section in the text and to the number within each section